CISTERCIAN FATHERS SERIES: NUMBER SEVENTY-ONE

Aelred of Rievaulx

THE LIVES OF THE NORTHERN SAINTS

D1447188

CISTERCIAN FATHER SERIES: NUMBER SEVENTY-ONE

Aelred of Rievaulx
The Lives of the
Northern Saints

Translated by
Jane Patricia Freeland

Edited, with an Introduction and Notes, by
Marsha L. Dutton

CISTERCIAN PUBLICATIONS
Kalamazoo, Michigan

The work of Cistercian Publications is made possible by support from Western Michigan University to The Institute of Cistercian Studies.

Aelred [Ethelred] of Rievaulx (1110–1167)

Library of Congress: Cataloging-in-Publication Data

Aelred, of Rievaulx, Saint, 1110–1167.
    Aelred of Rievaulx : the lives of the northern saints / translated by Jane Patricia Freeland ; Introduction and notes by Marsha L. Dutton.
      p.   cm. —— (Cistercian fathers series ; no. 71)
    Includes bibliographical references and index.
    ISBN-13: 978-0-87907-471-5
    ISBN-10: 0-87907-471-X
      1. Aelred, of Rievaulx, Saint, 1110–1167.   2. Ninian, Saint, d. 432?
3. Christian saints——United Kingdom——Biography.   I. Freeland, Jane Patricia,
1910–   II. Title.   III. Series.

BR1710.A35 2006
274.1'030922——dc22
[B]   2006023377

The editors dedicate this volume to the memory of

D. Martin Jenni

musician, scholar, and friend
who guided and moved many by his
music, erudition, generosity, and faith

1931–2006

Table of Contents

List of Abbreviations

GENERAL ABBREVIATIONS

a.	*ante*, before
Add.	Additional
Bede, HE	Bede, *Historia Ecclesiastica Gentis Anglorum*
BL	British Library
c.	*circa*, about
ca.; cc.	*capitulum*, chapter; chapters
CCC	Corpus Christi College (Cambridge University)
cf.	compare
cons.	consecrated
d.	died
Diss.	dissertation
ed.	editor / edited by
el.	elected
Ep(p)	*Epistola(e)*, Letter(s)
Epil	Epilogue
Hom	*Homilia*, homily
intro.	introduction / introduced by
Lat	Latin
MS.	manuscript
n; nn	Note; notes

n.d.	no date
nr.	number
n.v.	no volume
om.	omitted
ocso	Cistercian Order of the Strict Observance
Pref	*Prefatio*, Preface
Prol	*Prologus*, Prologue
rpt.	Reprint
S; Ss	*Sermo(nes)*, sermon(s)
s.a.	*sub annum*, 'under the year'
SUNY	State University of New York
Tract	*Tractatus*, tractate
trans.	translator / translated by
UK	United Kingdom
vol.; vols.	volume; volumes
Vulg	Vulgate

WORKS, SERIES, AND JOURNALS

ABR	*American Benedictine Review*
CCCM	Corpus Christianorum, Continuatio Mediaevalis
CF	Cistercian Fathers series. Spencer, Washington, DC, Kalamazoo, 1970–
Cîteaux	*Cîteaux: Commentarii Cistercienses; Cîteaux in de Nederlanden.* Westmalle, Belgium; Nuits-Saints-Georges, France, 1950–
Coll	*Collectanea cisterciensia; Collectanea o.c.r.*
CS	Cistercian Studies series
CSQ	*Cistercian Studies / Cistercian Studies Quarterly*
DNB	*Dictionary of National Biography*

HE	Bede, *Historia Ecclesiastica*. Ed. and trans. Bertram Colgrave and R. A. B. Mynors. *Bede's Ecclesiastical History of the English People*. Oxford: Clarendon Press, 1969.
MGH	Monumenta Germaniae Historica
PL	J.-P. Migne, *Patrologiae cursus completus, series latina*. 221 vols. Paris, 1844–64.
Raine	James Raine, ed. *The Priory of Hexham: Its Chroniclers, Endowments, and Annals*. 2 vols. Surtees Society 44. Durham: Andrews and Co., 1864.
RB	*Regula monachorum Sancti Benedicti, Rule of Saint Benedict*

WORKS OF AELRED OF RIEVAULX

Asspt	*Sermo in assumptione b. Mariae*
Bello stand	*De bello standardii*
Ep H	*Epistle to Henry II*
Gen Angl	*Genealogia regum Anglorum*
Iesu	*De Iesu puero duodenni*
Inst incl	*De institutione inclusarum*
Lam D	*Lamentatio David Regis Scotie*
Mira	*De quodam miraculum mirabile (= De sanctimoniali de Watton)*
Nat M	*Sermo in nativitate sanctae Mariae*
Oner	*Sermones de oneribus*
Orat past	*Oratio pastoralis*
OS	*Sermo in festivitate omnium sanctorum*
Palm	*Sermo in ramis palmarum*
PP	*Sermo in natali sanctorum apostolorum Petri et Pauli*
Pur	*Sermo in purificatione sanctae Mariae*
Spec car	*Speculum caritatis*

Spir amic   *De spiritali amicitia*
SS Hag   *De sanctis ecclesiae Hagulstadensis*
Synodo   *Sermo ad clerum in synodo Trecensi*
Trans   *Sermo in translacione sancti Edwardi confessoris*
Vita E   *Vita sancti Edwardi*
Vita N   *Vita sancti Niniani*

WORKS OF WALTER DANIEL

Ep M   *Epistola ad Mauriciam*
Lam   *Lamentacio Aelredo*
Vita A   *Vita Aelredi*

WORKS OF AUGUSTINE OF HIPPO

Civ Dei   *De Civitate Dei*
Conf   *Confessiones*
Doc   *De doctrina Christiana*
Enarr   *Enarrationes in Psalmos*

WORKS OF RICHARD OF HEXHAM

Acts   *Acts of King Stephen and the Battle of the Standard*
History   *History of the Church of Hexham*

WORKS OF SYMEON OF DURHAM

Church   *Libellvs de exordio atqve procvrsv istivs, hoc est Dvn-helmensis, ecclesie*
Kings   *Historia regum*

SCRIPTURAL ABBREVIATIONS

2 Chr	2 Chronicles
Col	Colossians
1 Cor	First Corinthians
2 Cor	Second Corinthians
Dn	Daniel
Dt	Deuteronomy
Eph	Ephesians
Ex	Exodus
Ez	Ezekiel
Gal	Galatians
Gn	Genesis
Hab	Habakkuk
Heb	Hebrews
Hos	Hosea
Is	Isaiah
Jas	James
Jb	Job
Jon	Jonah
Jdt	Judith
Jr	Jeremiah
Jn	John
1 Jn	1 John
Jos	Joshua
1 K	1 Kings
2 K	2 Kings
Lk	Luke
Lam	Lamentations
Mal	Malachi

Mk	Mark
Mt	Matthew
Nm	Numbers
Phil	Philippians
Prv	Proverbs
Ps(s)	Psalms
1 Pt	1 Peter
Rom	Romans
Rv	Revelation
Sg	Song of Songs
Si	Sirach (Ecclesiasticus)
1 Sm	1 Samuel
2 Sm	2 Samuel
Tb	Tobit
Ti	Titus
1 Tm	1 Timothy
2 Tm	2 Timothy
Ws	Wisdom

A Mirror
for Christian England[1]

B Y ANCESTRY AND ATTACHMENT Aelred of Rievaulx (1110–1167) was a child of the North of England, probably descended from one of those who carried Saint Cuthbert's body from Holy Island to Chester-le-Street and finally to Durham Cathedral.[2] In the mid-eleventh century his great-grandfather, Alfred son of Westou, was sacristan of that cathedral and so caretaker of Cuthbert's tomb. Alfred's son Eilaf, Aelred's grandfather, was a cathedral canon and treasurer of the monastery until 1083, when the new bishop of Durham, William of Saint Carileph, required

[1] I am grateful for a grant from the Summer Seminars and Institutes Program, Division of Educational Programs of the National Endowment for the Humanities, an independent federal agency, and to Paul E. Szarmach and Timothy Graham for the opportunity to study the manuscripts of Aelred's historical works as a participant in the 2000 NEH Summer Seminar in Anglo-Saxon Manuscripts and Texts at the British Library. I also thank the librarians and staff of the manuscript collections in the British Library, the Bodleian Library, the Cambridge University Library, the Parker Library of Corpus Christi College, Cambridge, and the Old Library of Jesus College Cambridge for their assistance. For assistance on biblical, historical, historiographical, and linguistic questions I thank Judith C. Avery, Fr Elias Dietz OCSO, E. Rozanne Elder, Carole Hutchison, Martin Jenni, R. T. Lenaghan, Joanne Pierce, Fr Chrysogonus Waddell OCSO, and Lorraine Wochna; for help in research and editing I thank F. Tyler Sergent, David A. Stuckey, and David J. Voelker. I owe particular gratitude to David Bullock for his assistance in compiling the indices to the volume. But above all I am grateful to Sr Jane Patricia Freeland for her erudition, graceful translations, and patient friendship.

[2] The identity of those who bore Cuthbert's body on its long journey is uncertain. Meryl Foster refers to 'the last oblates of Lindisfarne' ('Custodians', 57). Squire speaks of 'a little party of clerics and their families' (*Aelred of Rievaulx*, 5). Full references to all citations appear in the Bibliography, 123–129 below, using short titles or abbreviations from the list of Abbreviations, ix–xiv above.

married priests to choose between their wives and their positions at the cathedral. Leaving Durham—with his wife and children— Eilaf took up his father's benefice in the church of Saint Andrew at Hexham. One of Eilaf's sons, Aldred, later returned to Durham to become a monk there, and another son, Aelred's father Eilaf, died in the monastery in Durham in 1138. Aelred himself, one of three sons and perhaps a daughter born to Eilaf and his wife, probably studied in the cathedral school of Durham or York before spending ten years in the court of King David I of Scotland (r. 1124–1153).

Aelred's own life began in Hexham, where in 634 Saint Wilfrid had founded the church of Saint Andrew. During the centuries of viking raids Hexham and Saint Andrew's, like so much else of northern England, had suffered such depredations that the evidence of those horrors endured long after descendents of the Vikings had become peaceful subjects and, in some cases, even kings of England. Memories transmitted from parent to child colored Aelred's narratives of the history of England. In *Genealogy of the Kings of the English* he repeatedly writes of these kings' resistance to the Vikings, and in *The Saints of Hexham* he describes the destruction they wrought in the words and with the emotion of biblical authors grieving for the loss of Jerusalem:

> After the devastation of the Northumbrians, which the Danes lamentably brought about on their invasions into England, what happened to the other churches happened also to Hexham. To use the prophet's words, she lay groaning for a long time without a priest, without ephod or teraphim.[3] Then she wept bitterly in the night, tears on her cheeks.[4] Fire consumed everything; that renowned library that the holy bishop [Acca] had founded perished entirely. . . . the sacred places [were] laid waste by the savagery of the barbarians.[5]

This devastation was for Aelred not merely part of the historical record but a matter of personal consequence. When in 1083 Eilaf

[3] Hos 3:4.
[4] Lam 1:2.
[5] SS Hag 11.

and his family retreated from the great cathedral of Durham to Hexham, they found only ruins in place of the once beautiful church that Wilfrid had built and adorned. Aelred's account suggests that the family at first struggled merely to survive, but that in time Eilaf began to rebuild the church:

> When the man came to the place he found everything desolate, the walls of the roofless church overgrown with grass and made terrible by the encroaching forest. Ravaged by wear, rain, and storms, it retained nothing of its former beauty. The land was so desolate that for almost two years he sustained himself and his family only by hunting and fowling. Determined to restore the church, he began at the east end, where he erected an altar and fitted it out properly for the heavenly sacrifice.[6]

When Eilaf died his sons, Eilaf and Aldred, carried on the work of rebuilding the church, until in 1112 or 1113 the archbishop of York gave the now-restored church into the care of augustinian canons.

In Hexham today the memory of Alfred son of Westou and the two Eilafs who served as priests of the church of Saint Andrew has all but disappeared, and the church they rebuilt has been mostly replaced by the church erected in the twelfth and thirteenth centuries by the canons who replaced them. But on the south wall of the south transept of the church, beside the canons' graceful thirteenth-century night stairs, a plaque identifies Saint Wilfrid as the founder of the church, then lists the bishops, provosts, priests, and priors associated with the church before 1536. The list includes the name of three priests: ÆLFRED WESTOU 1021; EILAF LARWA 1042–1100; EILAF HIS SON, OB[IT] 1138. These are Aelred's great-grandfather, grandfather, and father.[7]

As Aelred's childhood and youth took much of their meaning from his family's connection to Cuthbert, Durham, and Hexham, the center of his adult life was his monastic conversion and his thirty-three years as a monk and abbot of the great cistercian abbey of Rievaulx. Founded in 1132 by Walter Espec a few miles from

---

[6] SS Hag 11.

[7] I am most grateful to Collin Dallison of Hexham for his assistance in clarifying my understanding of the medieval history of Hexham.

his hereditary castle at Helmsley, Rievaulx was the second cistercian monastery in England, founded by monks from the french abbey of Clairvaux under the leadership of William, himself from York-shire and, at Clairvaux, where he entered monastic life, secretary to the great abbot Bernard. If the new foundation was to thrive, it needed english monks, so when Aelred entered in 1134 the com-munity must have welcomed him warmly. Indeed Walter Daniel, the author of the 1167 *Life of Aelred of Rievaulx*, implies as much in his account of Aelred's entry: 'Today as yesterday the prior, with the guestmaster and the gate keeper and a great company of the brethren, hasten to him to do him honor. . . . He agrees at last to become a monk. They all rejoice, and all are glad together.'[8]

When Aelred took the journey in 1132 that concluded with his entry into Rievaulx, he first stopped in York to visit its arch-bishop, Thurstan, a visit that Walter Daniel explains as connected with an unidentified mission for King David. But the fact that Aelred's journey took him from David's court at Roxburgh[9] to York to Rievaulx to Helmsley—where he spent a night in Walter Espec's castle—and then back to Rievaulx as a postulant suggests not impulse but intention. The way that led him to monastic con-version seems likely to have been smoothed by the connections that linked four men to one another, to him, and to the Cistercian Order and the founding of Rievaulx: Archbishop Thurstan of York; King David I of Scotland; Walter Espec; and Abbot Bernard of Clairvaux.

David and Thurstan had ample reason for interaction, not only because of Thurstan's claim to authority over the church in Scotland but also because of their mutual support of augustinian priories.[10] In 1112 or 1113 Archbishop Thomas, Thurstan's predecessor at York, had introduced the augustinian canons at Hexham. When Thurstan succeeded to the see in 1114 he installed as the first prior of that small community Aschatil, a canon from Saint Mary's, Huntingdon;[11] Thurstan showed generous attention to the canons of Hexham

<hr/>

[8] Vita A 7; CF 57:100.

[9] Roxburgh, the old scottish capital, was near Kelso, about halfway between Edinburgh and Newcastle.

[10] Nicholl, *Thurstan*, 129; Dutton, 'Conversion and Vocation', 39.

[11] Cf. Aelred, SS Hag 11. Symeon of Durham says that Thomas introduced the canons in 1112 (*Kings* 193).

throughout his life. David was also a patron of augustinian canons at Aldgate, Llanthony, Jedburgh, and Cambuskenneth.[12] As David had become earl of Huntingdon in 1113 through his marriage to Matilda of Senlis,[13] he may have known Aschatil before he moved to Hexham; John of Hexham suggests that there was a cordial relationship between David and the Hexham canons.[14] Walter Espec, one of David's chief norman supporters, was also a patron to augustinian communities. In 1122 he provided the land for the foundation of Kirkham Priory, not far from Rievaulx on the banks of the River Derwent; in 1134 David's stepson Waldef became prior of Kirkham.

In addition to being patrons to augustinian houses, Thurstan, David, and Walter were all involved with the settlement of Cistercians in Yorkshire in the early 1130s. Thurstan had a particular interest in the young Cistercian Order because of having been in the company of Pope Callixtus II in 1119 when Callixtus approved the cistercian founding document, the *Carta Caritatis*. In the early 1130s Thurstan participated in the negotiations among Bernard of Clairvaux, King Henry I of England, and Walter Espec that resulted in the coming of monks from Clairvaux to Yorkshire. At about the same time he allowed a group of benedictine monks who had left Saint Mary's Abbey, York, to settle on land he owned near Ripon; in 1135 the new monastic house was incorporated into the Cistercian Order in the filiation of Clairvaux, becoming Fountains Abbey. David too may have supported both Rievaulx and Fountains in their early years. In 1134 Bernard wrote to request David's assistance to the monks at what would become Fountains Abbey, recalling his earlier generosity: 'the brethren at Rievaulx first knew the effects of your mercy. You opened to them the treasury of your good will and anointed them with the oil of your compassion and kindness.[15] Of course David's support to Rievaulx may have begun after and indeed resulted from Aelred's entry there rather than preceding it.

---

[12] Barrow, *Kingdom of the Scots*, 177–180; cf. Aelred, Lam D 2; here CF 56:49.

[13] Matilda (c. 1072–1131) was married to Simon of Senlis (St Liz), count of Huntingdon (d. c. 1111).

[14] John of Hexham, 'Prior John's Continuation', 115–116; cf. Dutton, 'Conversion and Vocation', 40.

[15] Bernard, Ep 69; SBOp 8:478–479, here 478.

These four men's interrelationships and mutual support for religious foundations in Yorkshire make it likely that Aelred's passage from Hexham to Roxburgh to Rievaulx and his entry to monastic life there derived some advantage from their friendship for him. He in turn conveyed his respect and affection for them in his works: in the preface addressed to Bernard in his first work, *Mirror of Charity*; in his acknowledgment of 'the help of the venerable Archbishop Thurstan' in the founding of Fountains and the encomium to Walter, both in *Battle of the Standard* and in his lamentation for the death of David in *Lament for David, King of the Scots*.[16]

As a new monk, Aelred had a great deal to offer his brothers at Rievaulx. Although, according to Walter Daniel, Aelred excelled in those things that matter most in a monk's life—prayer, meditation, and manual labor—he also brought from the scottish court skills particularly valuable for the quickly growing community. Not only was he fluent in English, Latin, and French, but he also had experience and perhaps a natural talent for diplomacy, as well as an ability to combine authority with humility, financial acumen with profound spirituality, and administrative efficiency with compassion and human understanding. Walter reports that the abbot of Rievaulx quickly began to consult with Aelred and to depend on his advice:

> His abbot, the lord William . . . determined to admit
> him to the intimacies of his counsel and to the discussion
> of matters closely affecting the household of Rievaulx.
> He discovered that Aelred was ten times as wise and
> prudent as he had supposed, and that he revealed an
> unexpected ease in the solution of hard, difficult and
> important problems. . . . he was like a second Daniel in
> disentangling cases and coming to a prudent decision.[17]

In 1142 Aelred represented Abbot William in a party of northern prelates journeying to Rome to appeal to Pope Innocent II for the removal of William Fitzherbert, a nephew of King Stephen, from the archbishopric of York. They carried with them a letter to

[16] Aelred, Spec car Pref; CF 17:73–75; Bello stand 2, CF 56:249–350; Lam D, CF 56:45–70.
[17] Vita A 14; CF 57:106–107.

Innocent from Bernard, who had interested himself in the matter.[18] After returning from Rome Aelred became novice master at Rievaulx and then founding abbot of Rievaulx's third daughter house, Saint Lawrence of Revesby. Walter Daniel reports his success in that office: 'And so the servant of the Lord . . . made his house rich and fruitful. Within, the religious life waxed every hour and grew day by day; without, possessions increased and gave a regular return in money and means for all kinds of equipment.'[19]

Aelred remained at Revesby for four years, until in 1147 the monks of Rievaulx elected him their abbot. There he stayed until his death, building Rievaulx into the greatest of the english cistercian abbeys, rich in people, property, influence, and the life of the spirit. Walter Daniel credits him with making Rievaulx 'the home of piety and peace, the abode of perfect love of God and neighbor' and 'the mother of mercy'. Walter adds that not only did Aelred welcome and protect 'the despised and rejected', the 'feeble in body and character', but he also declared their presence to be the great distinction of the monastery:

> Remember that 'we are all sojourners as were all our fathers,' and that it is the singular and supreme glory of the house of Rievaulx that above all else it teaches tolerance of the infirm and compassion with others in their necessities. And this is 'the testimony of our conscience', that this house is holy because it generates for its God sons who are peacemakers.[20]

Throughout the years that Aelred served as abbot at Revesby and Rievaulx he also wrote extensively—works of spiritual guidance and monastic teaching, works of advice or direction for anchoresses and kings, and works about the people and events of the North of England. His writing has won him recognition as one of the great spiritual teachers of the twelfth century, the author of

[18] David Knowles, 'The Case of St William of York', 82–83. Scholars generally assume that the group stopped at Clairvaux and that Aelred and Bernard met at that time; such a meeting certainly seems likely, but no record exists of it, and neither Bernard nor Aelred ever mentions it.
[19] Vita A 20; CF 57:110.
[20] Vita A 29; CF 57:118.

sermons and treatises about monastic life and charity, spiritual
friendship, and meditation on the life of Jesus of Nazareth. Through
and beyond the Middle Ages these works influenced writers such
as Jean de Meun, Peter of Blois, Bonaventure, Ludolph the Car-
thusian, and Ignatius of Loyola, all of whom either translated his
works, borrowed extensively from them, or incorporated passages
or ideas from his works into their own.[21] He is thus a fit companion
to such other cistercian abbots and writers of the twelfth century
as Bernard of Clairvaux, William of Saint Thierry, and Gilbert of
Hoyland.

What sets Aelred apart from all of these, however, is the satisfaction he obviously found in writing historical and hagiographical works alongside his sermons and treatises of spiritual guidance
and monastic education. Alone among the early Cistercians he
wrote numerous historical treatises, leaving at his death seven works
of history and spiritual biography. In addition to *The Battle of the
Standard*, his short account of the first great northern battle of the
Civil War between King Stephen and the Empress Matilda, he also
wrote about the five ancient bishops of Hexham as well as some
of the saints best remembered today in Scotland and the North of
England—Ninian, Cuthbert, Wilfrid, and John of Beverley.

In the historical works Aelred addressed the same topics and
themes that dominate his spiritual works. When he wrote about or
for kings he urged a devout faith and obedience to God's bishops
and saints, and he commended and encouraged such virtues as
chastity, generosity, humility, and justice. He considered royal power
to be grounded in the ruler's faith and virtue, and he gave his highest praise to kings who brought peace to England. So too when
he wrote for and about God's people in England, whether bishops,
nuns, canons, crippled girls, or Thames fishermen, he promised that
their faith, their trust, their humility, and their obedience would
bring them healing, blessing, and salvation.

In all that Aelred wrote he showed himself a spiritual teacher,
a moral advisor, a writer who considered himself to be intimately
related to all the people of England. Because he was one of them,
he understood their lives and experiences and knew himself com-

[21] Fleming, *Reason and the Lover*, 76–82; Hoste, *Bibliotheca Aelrediana*, 143;
Delhaye, 'Deux adaptations', 308–311; Dutton, 'The Cistercian Source', 157–
168.

staff protected the fleeing disciple lest he be swallowed up in the billows. You commanded the sea and the winds to dispel your disciples' fear; Ninian's power restrained the winds and the sea so that the lad might reach the shore he longed for.[32]

While Aelred here identifies Ninian with Christ, showing his life as *imitatio Christi*,[33] he also associates the sinful youth with Saint Peter, indicating that at all times those who call upon God's agents are numbered among the saints. Thus *Ninian* exalts not only the memory and enduring power of this early saint of Britain but also the humility and faith of those who found in him healing as well as illumination, physical well-being and with it the light and truth of God.

For Aelred's Ninian is a man of learning and divine vision as well as of healing power, a contemplative as well as a missionary. He models the life of active charity, but through his search for truth he also exemplifies the contemplative life. While both Bede and Aelred celebrate him for his active apostleship at Whithorn, both also remember him as a seeker for knowledge and the understanding of Scripture. Describing Ninian's search in the language of the *Song of Songs*, a book he quotes nowhere else in the historical works, Aelred identifies Ninian's love of learning, which led him as a youth to study in Rome, with the contemplative search for Christ as truth and wisdom.[34] At the end of Ninian's life, his active and contemplative lives become one in the sight of God, and Christ himself welcomes him to beatitude:

> Christ consoled him, saying, 'Arise, hasten, my beloved, my dove, and come.' 'Arise, my beloved', he said; 'arise, my dove; arise by your understanding, hasten onward by your desire, come by your steadfast love.' These words

[32] Vita N 10.

[33] Thomas Heffernan emphasizes 'the medieval understanding that the saint's life is the perfect *imitatio Christi*' (*Sacred Biography*, 20).

[34] Aelred's association of learning with the contemplative search for wisdom and the eternal sight of the face of God is characteristic of early cistercian thought, epitomized by William of Saint-Thierry's statement of reason and love as the two eyes that unite in the single sight of God (Nat am 3.21; PL 184:393; CF 30:77–78).

were clearly appropriate to the blessed man, as he was
the bridegroom's friend to whom the heavenly bridegroom had entrusted his bride, to whom he had revealed
his secrets, to whom he had opened his treasures.[35]

To the Christians of Galloway Aelred thus presents a historical
figure, a man of God, a missionary and builder of churches, a man
of vision, charity, and power, and a lover of truth. As in his life
Ninian sought God's wisdom, Aelred says, he also manifested God's
loving-kindness and power, enabling the people to whom he was
Christ's apostle to come through him to Christ in trust and faith.

On the Saints of Hexham

The treatise *On the Saints of Hexham* is thought to have originated
as a homily for the augustinian canons at Hexham, Aelred's boyhood
home, for regular use on the annual 3 March celebration of the
1155 translation of the relics of their saints, Eata, Acca, Alchmund,
Frethbert, and Tilbert. Aelred pays special attention to the history
of the town and its church as well as to its saints, noting that the
church, 'founded under the very earliest kings, has long been resplendent with the dignity of the seat of a bishop'.[36]
    There has been some doubt about the authorship of *Hexham*,
because it contains no textual identification of the author, who
several times seems to identify himself as a member of the Hexham
community: 'This festival is ours, especially for us who live in this
very holy place under the patronage of [these saints]'.[37] Both
Mabillon and the *Acta Sanctorum* thus identify the author as 'an
anonymous regular canon, in the mid-twelfth century'.[38] James
Raine, nineteenth-century editor of *Hexham*, regards as conclusive
the identification of Aelred as author in the incipits of the two
principal manuscripts of the work: 'I conceive that it is by Aelred,
abbat of Rievaulx, on the basis of manuscript ascription'. He then

---

[35] Vita N 11; see Sg 2:10.
[36] SS Hag Prol.
[37] SS Hag Prol.
[38] 'Auctore anonymo canonico regulari, medio sæculo xii' (*Acta SS. Ord. S.B.*,
sæc. Iii., para i. [ed. 1734]), cited from Raine, *Priory*, 173 n. c.

explains how to make sense of the passages that seem to indicate a Hexham canon as the author:

> We must look upon the author as . . . choosing words which the canon who recited them to his brethren could use with the most perfect propriety on each recurring anniversary of their festive day. Aelred, in fact, was drawing up a Legend for the canons and for future use.[39]

The work describes the translation of the saints at Hexham as a past event, and Walter Daniel does not mention Aelred's having written this work or preached at Hexham. But Aelred Squire suggests, and other scholars have agreed, that the nucleus of the book 'is a sermon Aelred preached at Hexham on 3 March 1155, when the bones in which his father and uncle had interested themselves were translated to new shrines'.[40] A reference in the text to the church's 'wonderful stone work—as you see before you' and the assertion that 'we rightly believe that [Saint Wilfrid] is participating in this very holy festival'[41] show that it was at least in part prepared for public presentation at Hexham.

Internal evidence supports the traditional attribution to Aelred. In the body of the work the writer sometimes seems to distinguish between himself and the Hexham canons, saying of Saint Acca 'you possess his chasuble' and recalling that during the Civil War 'our men, who were with the king, were moved by pity to transport many whom they had snatched from their power to Hexham'.[42] Further, the writer's references to his own childhood in Hexham (though impersonally phrased), his expressions of familiarity with and affection for the first canons who came there, and his fund of stories about the members of his family make the identification too appealing to resist. But that appeal rests in some ways on the particular charm and nostalgic tone of the work, elements that set

---

[39] Raine, *Priory*, 173–174 nn. a, d. Both Oxford MS. Laud 668 and BL MS. Add. 38,816 name Aelred as author; BL MS. Cotton Vitellius A.XX, which contains a severely abbreviated version of the work, names no author.

[40] Squire, *Aelred of Rievaulx*, 112.

[41] SS Hag Prol.

[42] SS Hag 6, 5.

it stylistically apart from Aelred's other works. It echoes with places known and stories heard in childhood, shared jokes and experiences of youth. It has a curiously old-fashioned air as saints ride in on horseback, and it is full of family reminiscences recalled in laughter.

Hexham also resembles Aelred's other hagiographical works in its exhortation to readers or listeners to imitate the humility and faith of those earlier residents of Hexham who trusted in their saints. Often here as in those other works it is the most humble who benefit most from the saints' power. In one case a youth condemned to death for theft prays 'to our common refuge—that is to say, to Saint Wilfrid—and to the other patron saints of this church'. As the executioner prepares to strike, the boy cries out, 'Help me now, Wilfrid, because if you don't now, soon you won't be able to'. As laughter fills the place, delaying the executioner's stroke, 'two young men, astride very swift horses, raced up. Presenting surety . . . they snatched the youth away from death, freed him from his chains, and allowed him to go away free'.

The moral Aelred draws here is like that in *Ninian*: trust in God and his saints brings aid in all necessity: 'If we should be bound by the chains of some wicked habit . . . let us beg the help of these saints with our eyes raised to heaven and our tears falling copiously. We know that they will take up arms and shields and arise to help us'. Yet the historical event and its place in local memory at once recur, 'This miracle became known to so many that the youth's words, proven effective in so great an extremity, became a common adage among all the people'.[43]

Many such stories in this work suggest that Aelred heard them as a boy in Hexham. So too does his occasional inclusion of Cuthbert and Wilfrid, even though neither was officially among the saints of the place. Aelred's family had a particular devotion to Cuthbert, dating perhaps to the presence of one of their ancestors within the cuthbertian community on Lindisfarne. The ninth-century bishopric of Wilfrid at Hexham remained in the active memory of the local residents, and the churches he erected there play their part in the miracles of this work. Cuthbert and Wilfrid

[43] SS Hag 1.

were the great patrons of the church of Hexham; for Aelred any celebration of its saints required their presence.

One of Aelred's favorite stories in this work has more to do with Cuthbert and Wilfrid than with the other five bishops. When Malcolm III of Scotland attacked Hexham, Aelred writes, the people fled for protection to the church: 'Some appealed with groans and outcries to Wilfrid, some to Cuthbert, some to Acca, and not a few to Alchmund.' During the night in a vision the priest of the church sees two bishops 'on horseback, approaching the church from the south'. Dismounting and leaving their horses in the priest's care, they go to the church to pray, then, on their return, promise to save the town by extending a net 'from the source of the River Tyne to its mouth'.

When the priest asks who they are, the leader explains: 'I am called Wilfrid, and see, here with me is Saint Cuthbert. I brought him with me as I passed Durham, so that we might come at the same time to our brothers who rest in this church and preserve this place and its people'. And indeed at dawn 'A kind of cloud' arose out of the west and covered the river, swallowing up the scottish soldiers; a sudden flood kept Malcolm there for three days more, until at last, 'coming to himself', he said, 'What are we doing? Let us withdraw from here, for these houses are holy'.[44]

Aelred first mentions this story in the work's prologue; warning of the power of the saints against 'our spiritual enemies', he urges his audience to 'recall how powerfully they once snatched a helpless people, besieged in this church, out of the hand of those more powerful'.[45] Thus at the same time that the narrative proves the power of those who protected Hexham in the past and continue to do so in the present, it seems also to reflect the memory of rainy northumbrian afternoons, with small boys listening again and again to stories worn soft by time.

---

[44] SS Hag 2. The collaborative effort of Cuthbert and Wilfrid in two of the miracles in this work is particularly striking in light of the conflict between their two cults in the anglo-saxon period; see David Rollason, 'Hagiography and Politics', 105. As in the other historical works, especially Gen Angl, Aelred insists here that the great saints of anglo-saxon England continue to watch over and protect the English even after the Conquest; see Gen Angl 7, 12; CF 56:79–81, 90–92.

[45] SS Hag Prol.

The true saints of Hexham are the five bishops who served
and were buried there, ancient men largely unknown even in the
twelfth century. Although with their individuality largely buried
in the past they tend in this work to act in concert, Aelred recounts
a few stories featuring them as individuals. Acca, successor to
Wilfrid, was the most active of these saints, the one best known
for his healing of the sick and, especially, the blind. So when a man
named Raven went blind, on 'the birthday of the most blessed Acca
. . . the day on which he passed joyously from this corporeal darkness to the splendor of true light', Raven turned to the saint and
was healed. Aelred explicates this miracle's meaning when he con-
cludes with an exhortation like the one at the beginning of the
work: 'Would that we, dearest brothers, might in dangers to our
souls implore his aid with the same faith, equal devotion, and no
less hope. . . .'[46]

The miracles of this work include several exercised by the saints
in self-protection against Aelred's own ancestors, who appear in
the work as not only struggling to rebuild the decayed fabric of
the church but also occasionally attempting to keep for themselves
some fragments of the saints' relics. Within the narrative these
stories function to prove the endurance of the saints' power into
modern times. At the same time they reveal something of the
personality of Aelred, who here shows a lively and relaxed wit that
leavens his moral purpose with homely recollection and laughter.
If indeed this work began as a homily, it is no wonder that he was
a popular preacher.

The most memorable of the forebears of Aelred seen in *Hexham*
is his great-grandfather, Alfred son of Westou, remembered as an
enthusiastic collector of relics and credited with having brought
the bones of Aelred's favorite historian, the Venerable Bede, to
Durham Cathedral, placing them beside those of Cuthbert. Aelred
explains Alfred's avocation as evidence of his faith, his reverence
for the saints, and his reaction to the viking raids on Northumbria:
'Prompted by divine revelation, as he passed through the sacred
places laid waste by the savagery of the barbarians, he took the
relics of many saints from their burial places and transferred them
to the church at Durham.' Among those Alfred once attempted

[46] SS Hag 7.

unsuccessfully to collect, Aelred explains, were those of Acca at Hexham, but 'foreseeing . . . what sacredness and honor this church was to have, he was unwilling, or unable, to take away these sacred relics. He concealed them decently inside the church.'[47] The authorial aside 'or unable' preserves a rare echo here of Aelred's voice as preacher and *raconteur*.

In the work's final story Aelred once more shows the continued power of the Hexham saints into the recent past, that of his own boyhood and the early years of the Augustinians at Hexham. When the 'overbearing and proud' clergy of York attempted to acquire the relics of Eata, arguing that 'the undistinguished church at Hexham possessed five bishops while York had not even one', Archbishop Thomas II (1108–1114) yielded, knowing the safety of such a raid on Hexham: 'There was no one to refuse them, no one to open the mouth and raise an alarm'. And indeed when the clergy and the archbishop came for the bones they had selected, the canons' efforts at resistance had no effect.

At night, however, Eata appeared with his staff to the archbishop and chastised him, then twice struck him with the staff. In the morning Thomas promised 'that he would never again attempt anything of this kind' and begged prayers from the canons. Four days later, Aelred notes, he was finally well enough to return to York.[48] *Hexham* ends here, with this final proof of the saints' power.

While this story is an appropriate ending to the themes of the treatise, its abrupt finish, without his usual request that his audience pray for him and a doxology, suggests either that a portion of the original manuscript has been lost or that Aelred left the work incomplete, perhaps in order that the canons might provide their own exordium and conclusion. He cannot have intended for the work to conclude as it does, especially give his careful balancing elsewhere of each miracle of the past with an explanation of its present significance.

In *Hexham* Aelred shows saints of greater fierceness and less learning than Ninian, more ready to defend their episcopal dignity, even against other bishops, than to seek for right doctrine and scriptural understanding. But in both life and death they too are

---

[47] SS Hag 11.
[48] SS Hag 16.

shown as saving the deserving and the undeserving, forgiving those who offended, and manifesting God's grace to those who called on them. Like Ninian they not only healed but also illuminated, bringing God's light into the darkness of human sin. So Aelred celebrates them, through them remembering his own ancestors and, it seems, his childhood among the churches and saints of Hexham.

A Certain Wonderful Miracle

Aelred wrote *A Certain Wonderful Miracle* in about 1160, about a recent violent episode culminating in a series of miracles in the small gilbertine priory of Watton, near York. Aelred does not identify his intended audience, addressing him merely as 'most beloved Father' and 'my dearest friend'.[49] In the prologue to the work he declares his desire to share the miracles he has witnessed with someone who will trust his account. From the first to the last line of the work emphasizes 'the Lord's miracles, the clear signs of his divine loving-kindness' and 'the glory of Christ'.[50] The emotional weight of the work, however, is on the suffering of a girl grown to young adulthood among a community of women who neglected her, resented her, and finally brutally punished her when she became pregnant. Thus one of Aelred's purposes in writing was surely to warn of the dangers inherent in the structure of gilbertine monasteries, which combined women and men in a single community.[51]

---

[49] Mira Prol, Epil.

[50] Mira Prol, Epil.

[51] Golding, *Gilbert of Sempringham*, 33–38. Gilbertine monasticism began when Gilbert of Sempringham established a community in which twelve young women could live essentially as solitaries, served by lay sisters and later lay brothers. In 1147, after the cistercian General Chapter refused the gilbertine request for cistercian superiors, Gilbert added canons as priests and administrators. Understanding Gilbert's request for superiors as indicating a desire to be admitted into the Cistercian Order, scholars have sought to explain the cistercian refusal, speculating for example that the Order was unwilling to accept communities of women or that it was deterred by the poverty of the two small gilbertine priories that existed in 1147. Fr Chrysogonus Waddell OCSO has pointed out to me, however, that Gilbert asked not for incorporation of his priories into the Order but that the

Miracle (for 160 years known as *The Nun of Watton* from Migne's title, taken from the running head in Roger Twysden's seventeenth-century edition[52]) was written at about the same time as Aelred's other work about women in religious life, *On the Formation of Anchoresses*.[53] Both works combine a concern for women in new forms of religious life—gilbertine monasticism and anchoritism—with Aelred's usual hagiographical emphasis on God's loving-kindness for both the virtuous and the fallen. *Miracle*, however, is the story not of a saint but of a sinner. Further, the miracle of the work's title occurs only at the end of the narrative, which builds slowly through seduction, rape, pregnancy, battery, imprisonment, and yet more violence until in a series of visions Saint Henry Murdac and two assistants release the protagonist from her pregnancy and God releases her from her bonds.

Aelred begins *Miracle* in his usual fashion, stating his reason for writing: the importance of declaring God's action in human affairs. As in *Hexham*, he insists that miracles benefit not only the immediate recipients but also those who attend to them:

> To know and yet hide the Lord's miracles, the clear signs
> of his divine loving-kindness, is an aspect of sacrilege.
> For to deprive everyone of what can console people of
> the present, instruct those who come afterward, and
> increase the devotion of all is shameful.[54]

So this work, superficially a story of sexual wrongdoing and violent reprisal, shares the themes of Aelred's other hagiographical works: God's revelation through miracles of his loving-kindness and the

---

Order appoint superiors for them: *'ut curam domorum suarum manciparet custodie monachorum Cistercie'* (Foreville and Keir, *The Book of Saint Gilbert*, 40–41). Further, Fr Chrysogonus explains, the regulations of the Order forbade naming members of the Order as superiors in non-cistercian monasteries: *'Nam de extraneis ecclesiis abbatem sibi sumere, aut suos aliis ad hoc ipsum monachos dare Cisterciensibus non licet'* (Waddell, ed., *Narrative and Legislative Texts,* 282, 450–451).

[52] Roger Twysden, ed., *Historiæ Anglicanæ Scriptores* X:415–422; rpt. PL 195:789–796. The work is repeatedly referred to in its unique manuscript as *De quodam miraculum mirabili*.

[53] *Inst incl;* CCCM 1:635–82; trans. CF 2:41–102 as 'Rule of Life for a Recluse'.

[54] Mira 1.

effects of that revelation on human trust and hope. The horror within the narrative thus serves as the occasion for God to manifest his love.

The work begins with two stories praising the holiness of two groups of nuns at Watton: in the past—when John of Beverley was archbishop of York (705–718)—and in the present, in a gilbertine priory. The first story, taken from Bede's *Ecclesiastical History*, tells of John's miraculous healing of one of the eighth-century nuns.[55] The second one declares the contemplative blessings commonly experienced by the twelfth-century nuns. With these two stories Aelred establishes the divine favor in which the Watton nuns live while foreshadowing the more recent and much less expected blessing to the least deserving of their community.[56]

The story central to the treatise is a somber one. As Aelred recounts, a four-year-old girl introduced into Watton by Henry Murdac, archbishop of York (1147–1153), was throughout her childhood unable to accept the monastic regime. Nonetheless, once she reached the appropriate age she became a member of the community. She then met and became friendly with a handsome lay brother, who, after a time of growing familiarity, raped her: 'She is thrown down, her mouth is stopped lest she cry out, and, having been already debauched in mind, she is debauched in body'.[57] When she becomes pregnant, the man—rightfully fearing the nuns' rage—flees. When the nuns discover the girl's pregnancy, they whip and fetter her, then lure the young man back and force her to castrate him.

The violence of this chain of events emphasizes both the girl's need for mercy and the unlikelihood of her receiving it. But then comes the miracle that Aelred promised. As the girl lies in her cell, great with child and bound by both feet, Murdac appears to her accompanied by two women who deliver her child and take it away. Soon afterward 'two ministers of divine mercy come to her; the one . . . removing the chain that bound her so tightly'.[58]

Aelred voices his judgment on this miraculous deliverance in two roles, as both actor in and author of the narrative. As a figure

[55] Bede, HE 4.27–5.2.

[56] Freeman, 'Nuns in the Public Sphere', points out that the two stories also emphasize the virtues of friendship and communal charity significantly absent from the rest of the work.

[57] Mira 5.

[58] Mira 10.

within the narrative, after the two miracles take place he is consulted at Rievaulx and invited to Watton, where he examines the fetter remaining on the girl. Declaring to the nuns 'that without God's power she could not have been loosed from the others, nor could she be loosed from this one',[59] he advises that she be left to God and returns to Rievaulx. Soon afterward God's judgment appears when the remaining fetter also falls. Murdac, the heavenly visitors, and God thus act in concert to release the girl from her pregnancy, bonds, and sin, and Aelred serves as witness to the authenticity of the events. By explaining the meaning of the divine acts to the nuns and to his readers, Aelred ensures that both the participants in the events and his audience will understand them.

Aelred's concern goes beyond the miraculous resolution of the young nun's plight, extending to the well-being of the community and perhaps to their Order, suggesting the implications of the founder's failure adequately to anticipate such danger and to protect his communities from it. Early in the work Aelred points to the risk posed to women in gilbertine communities by the structure of their life. Although he insists on the virtue of the older nuns, he rages over the community's lack of care for their young ward:

> Where then, Father Gilbert, was your vigilant concern
> for the keeping of discipline? Where were your many
> delicate devices for excluding occasions of sin? Where
> then was your concern—so prudent, so cautious, and so
> acute—your watch so faithful over each door, window,
> and corner that even evil spirits seemed to be denied
> access?[60]

Unwilling to reprove the community that he has already commended, Aelred expresses a qualified praise for them, explaining them as 'having the zeal of God although not according to knowledge'.[61] In view of Benedict's distinction between good and bad zeal in RB 72 and of the association Aelred makes in *Ninian* between

[59] Mira 11.

[60] Mira 4. Brian Golding sees the increased strictness of the gilbertine order in the thirteenth century as a direct consequence of *Miracle*, referring to the events Aelred recounts as 'a catalyst to institutional development' (*Gilbert of Sempringham*, 38).

[61] Mira 7.

the desire for learning and the love of God, this judgment on the nuns' lack of understanding indicates that despite their experience of 'heavenly contemplation' and 'indescribable ecstasies',[62] they have fallen short of wisdom.[63]

Aelred makes it clear that his narrative depends almost entirely on the explanations of members of the community, from their judgment of the young nun's character as a child and young woman to their brutality when they find her pregnant, to their vengeance on her rapist, to their fear when they find her fetters fallen. By repeating their explanations, essentially in their own words, he allows them tacitly to confess their fault toward their ward and sister, their lack of love, protection, and compassion, which gave her loveless years in childhood and exposed her and themselves to violence, shame, and misery.

At the same time Aelred demonstrates his own compassion for the girl, victim of Gilbert's and the community's carelessness, lack of foresight, and emotional neglect. As an advisor, he directs the older nuns to accept the loss of the chains as representing God's decision, and as an author he differentiates between the motives of the lovers: 'He was planning debauchment, but she said afterwards that she was thinking only of love'.[64] He shows the girl as accepting her brutal treatment by the nuns without complaint, and he evokes readers' pity on her when he writes of visiting her 'where she was sitting, shut in her cavern.'[65]

Most important, Aelred shows in this work as in both *Ninian* and *Hexham* that God extends his compassion not only to saints but also to ordinary fallen men and women, to wrong-doers as well as those filled with virtue. For while Aelred condemns the young nun's misdeeds, he insists that God shows her mercy: 'And truly the sinful woman moved the holy heart of Jesus with her grief and disgrace, and also with the abuse she suffered. . . . Let sinners hear, so that they never despair of the goodness of him who so exercises judgment as not to forget mercy'.[66] The echoes in the work of other wronged or sinning women, including Jacob's

---

[62] Mira 1.
[63] Cf. Raciti, 'Preferential Option'.
[64] Mira 3.
[65] Mira 11.
[66] Mira 8.

daughter Diana and the woman taken in adultery, place this adulterous daughter of Watton within a biblical context and recall God's age-old constancy in mercy. The work also resonates with the tone of those marian legends in which the Virgin Mary anticipates the sinner's need for mercy.[67]

The miraculous release of the young nun of Watton, like the miracles in *Ninian* and *Hexham*, serves Aelred as evidence of God's compassion for those who fall. As his advice to the community at Watton he records his judgment in Christ's words from Acts 10:15 and Matthew 16:19: 'What God has cleansed you must not call common, and her whom he has loosed you must not bind'.[68]

Aelred thus uses *Miracle* as a kind of parable with two messages. It warns of the sexual temptations inherent in the structure of gilbertine life, despite the holiness of many of the women in the Order. But its greater concern is that manifest in all Aelred's hagiographical works, declared in its title and its early proclamation that God's miracles are 'the clear signs of his divine loving-kindness'.[69] The argument of the work is God's love made visible to those broken in fear and lust and sin; its meaning is not human sin or divine wrath but divine love.

Ninian, *Hexham*, and *Miracle* all center in the manifestation of God's loving-kindness to ordinary men and women, more often than not those who show least desert but most need. Repeatedly Aelred declares that when humans are unable or unwilling to help themselves or one another, Christ hears their need and acts through the saints: 'Yours are these deeds, O Christ!'[70] He also shows the continuing bond between the saints and their earthly homes and relationships. Ninian works miracles of healing at his tomb, Wilfrid and Cuthbert come to Hexham to save its people, and Henry Murdac rescues the girl for whose suffering he is in part responsible. Aelred's saints exhibit a cistercian love of the place and its people, building and decorating their homes when they are alive

---

[67] Giles Constable notes, in 'Aelred of Rievaulx and the Nun of Watton', that 'no exactly comparable miracle appears' in the standard indices; he cites as the earliest analogue one in the marian miracles of Dominic of Evesham, from the early 1120s (212–213).

[68] Mira 11.

[69] Mira Prol.

[70] Vita N 10.

and refusing to allow their bones to be taken away after they are dead. But the saints themselves are not really the center of his works, and Aelred rarely suggests them as models for human behavior. Rather, they witness to God's enduring presence and attention to the needs of his people, through their miracles assuring hope, nourishing love, and confirming future gifts of joy.

A Mirror For Women

In the historical works as elsewhere Aelred presents women as partners with men; both sexes appear as models of virtue and faith and exemplifications of God's loving-kindness. Especially in the historical works, written primarily for non-cenobites, lay and clerical, both men and women appear as mirrors and *exempla* for kings, nuns, and pilgrims, for all sorts of sinners and saints.

Aelred's women range from such christian queens as Margaret of Scotland and her daughter, Henry I's Good Queen Maud, to nuns and anchoresses, from biblical figures to warriors and founders of cities. Indeed Aelred declares in *Spiritual Friendship* that God created women as men's equals, explaining the creation of Eve, the usual object of and rationalization for medieval misogyny, as evidence of the essential equality of all humans: 'It is beautiful that the second human being was taken from the side of the first, so that nature might teach that all are equal, as it were collateral, and that in human affairs there is neither superior nor inferior.'[71]

Most often, however, Aelred shows men and women to be co-workers for good or bad, a point he makes not by abstract statement but by a depiction of their parallel and often identical roles in the world. In *Miracle*, for example, he links men and women at each moment of the story, in virtue and wrongdoing, in fault and resolution. He blames both the young nun and her rapist, and he blames both Gilbert, who failed to protect his community, and the nuns, who exercised zeal rather than knowledge in their vengeance. Furthermore, when Archbishop Murdac visits the girl to release her from the consequences of her sin he comes in the company of

---

[71] Spir amic 1.57; CCCM 1:298–99; CF 5:62–63. For Aelred's discussion of God's creation of Adam and Eve as the first friends, see Dutton, 'Friendship and the Love of God', 25–27.

women, two heavenly midwives, but later two male figures release her from her chains. These two miracles suggest Aelred's conscious intention to show men and women at work together.

Aelred also praises the virtue and faith of individual women at Watton. He reveals God's acknowledgment of the nuns' merit when he tells of their contemplative blessings, he declares the certainty that all he recounts is true because of his confidence in their testimony, and he justifies that confidence by citing his own experience of finding women there who were 'powerful in wisdom and judgment, remarkable for holiness and much practice of regular discipline'.[72] What is more, he describes the young nun herself as attempting to resist her seducer and then, having failed to do so, acknowledging her fault, suffering her torments without complaint, and in the words of Jesus' own prayer accepting her tormentors' decision to release her to the man who ruined and then abandoned her: 'According to the will of heaven, so be it'.[73]

Throughout the historical works women also appear as leaders in virtue and faith while occupying social roles ranging from wife and mother to warrior and founder of cities. *Genealogy*, perhaps as a result of Aelred's profound familiarity with Bede's *Ecclesiastical History*, contains a number and variety of women.[74] Aelred begins the work by presenting to Henry II for his emulation his closest female royal ancestors, his mother, grandmother, and great-grandmother: 'You then, good Sir, are the son of the most illustrious Empress Matilda. Her mother was the most christian and excellent queen of the English, Matilda, daughter of the holy woman Margaret, queen of the Scots, who set sanctity of life above the luster of her name.'[75]

Again at the end of the work Aelred returns to Henry's female relatives, including other descendants of Edmund Ironside: his daughter-in-law Agatha, wife of his son, Edward Atheling, and their

---

[72] Mira 11.

[73] Mira 6.

[74] Catherine E. Karkov infers from the 'patriarchal nature of text, genealogy, and history' in the Hebrew Bible that 'The creation of history and culture was traditionally then no place for women', but she notes exceptions to that rule in, for example, Bede's *Ecclesiastical History* and Asser's *Life of Alfred* ('The Anglo-Saxon Genesis', 220, 224–227).

[75] Gen Angl 2; CF 56:72.

children, Margaret, Christina, and Edgar Atheling. Additional details from the family history, such as Margaret's marrying Malcolm, king of the Scots, and Christina's becoming a nun, establish Henry within a family as memorable for its women as for its men.[76]

Henry's grandmother, Queen Matilda, is especially important in this work, exemplifying christian charity for her brother, King David, and so for Aelred's readers, Henry among them. In praising her Aelred links her to one of the biblical women who saved her people: 'Anyone who wants to write about her wonderful renown and her strength of mind . . . will show us another Esther in our own time'.[77] To show 'the sort of woman she was toward Christ's poor', Aelred tells a story that he learned, he says, from David himself.

As a boy staying at the court of Henry I and Matilda, David once watched as his sister washed, dried, and kissed the feet of lepers. When warned of her husband's probable reaction to such acts, Matilda explained them as an expression of love for Christ: 'Who does not know that the feet of the eternal king should be preferred to the lips of a king who will die? Indeed I called you for this, my dearest brother, so that you would learn by my example to do the same. Take the basin then, and do what you see me doing'.[78] This lesson is the moral of the scene Aelred offers to his own royal listener, the grandson of Matilda and her mortal king.

The holiness of the queen in this story and her attempt to teach her young brother mirrors the holiness of the biblical women who loved Jesus and Aelred's direction to twelfth-century men and women to imitate them. In *Formation* he repeatedly directs the contemplative he addresses to kiss the feet of her infant spouse and her crucified lord, offering her as a model the women who washed or kissed Jesus' feet.[79] By showing Queen Matilda in *Genealogy* as a model for her brother and grandson, Aelred creates a modern-day parallel to the evangelical women who ministered to Jesus, their

[76] As Freeman notes, however, Aelred focuses on these women largely as mothers and to a lesser extent wives of the english kings, for the most part ignoring women's own experiences and activities while emphasizing their virtue, their role in establishing a 'moral genealogy' (*Narratives*, 70–85, here 82).

[77] Gen Angl 24; CF 56:119.

[78] Gen Angl 24; CF 56:120.

[79] Inst incl 31; CCCM 1:666; CF 2:86. Aelred's use of the pericope of the woman Jesus blesses because she has loved much (Lk 7:36–56) works as a *leitmotif* throughout the meditation on the past in this work.

eternal spouse and king. Finally both the queen and the women of the Old and New Testaments serve his readers as *exempla* of charity, humility, and faith.

Women representative of not only faith but also its reward in contemplative experience are most prominent in *Miracle* and *Formation*, Aelred's two works about religious women. In both works he balances warnings against the sexual temptation and danger experienced by uncloistered religious women with a recognition of the spiritual blessings those same women receive. *Miracle* combines an instance of the danger inherent in the structure of gilbertine double houses with celebration of the spiritual gifts of the gilbertine women at Watton.[80] The anchoress in *Formation* is both reminded of the risks she runs by talking to visitors at her window and praised as one inebriated by divine visitations. Aelred urges her to pursue these latter joys: 'how often he lifted up your mind from the things of earth and introduced it into the delights of heaven and the joys of Paradise. Turn all this over in your mind so that your spirit may go out wholly to him.'[81] Aelred consistently portrays women as recipients of contemplative vision and solace.

While these two late works express anxiety about the sexual dangers facing religious women outside traditional forms of monasticism, Aelred shows no such concern in his other works. While in his first work, *The Mirror of Charity*, he warns that monks sometimes come to desire virtuous women (as they may sometimes desire virtuous men), he says nothing of women's being equally tempted.[82] In *Spiritual Friendship* he names as friends to men not only Eve but Ruth and 'the young woman of Antioch', who escapes a brothel with help from a soldier; he never hints that these women risk sexual temptation. Further, unlike many other medieval authors, he does not blame women for men's desiring them. While he warns of the likely consequences of the natural attraction between men and women, his concern is not the attraction but its indulgence.

In addition to women set apart by vows of religion, by public acts of charity, or by contemplative experience, Aelred also writes of women remembered only as the mothers, wives, and daughters of english kings, women almost anonymous and yet remembered

[80] Aelred discusses the visionary experiences of the Watton nuns in Oner 2 (PL 195:370–372).
[81] Inst incl 32; CCCM 1:676; CF 2:96.
[82] Spec car 3.28.66–68; CCCM 1:136–37; CF 17:266–267.

and sometimes named in this work along with their male relatives as ancestors and relatives of Henry of Anjou. Aelred's frequent inclusion of royal wives and daughters reminds readers that sons are born of their mothers as well as of their fathers and that children may be daughters as well as sons. So he notes that 'King Edward lived in his kingdom twenty-four years and begot sons and daughters'[83] and 'His brother Æthelred, son of Edgar and the queen, succeeded him'.[84] He mentions the founding of monasteries for men and for women as equivalents, and when he tells of King Edward the Elder's founding 'a new monastery at Winchester', he adds 'and his mother, the very holy woman Ealhswith, built a monastery for virgins in the same city'.[85] Again, in *Edward* he describes the Confessor's queen, Edith, as a rare exception to the general depravity of her family, a rose born from thorns, taking flesh from her father but 'her schooling in holiness . . . from the spirit of God'.[86]

Not all of the women in these works represent religious or domestic life; others are remembered for their exercise of public or military power. Aelred ascribes particular influence to the great warrior and leader Æthelflæd, 'Lady of the Mercians', the daughter of Alfred the Great: 'In sex she was a woman, but in spirit and strength more a man. She constructed cities beyond those the king had built. . . . She displayed such courage that many called her king'.[87]

Anonymous women of unknown identity and situation also fill the leaves of Aelred's historical works, as recipients of miracles and sometimes as intercessors who effect the healing of those they love. In *Hexham* the sister of a cleric blinded for lack of belief successfully pleads with Acca to restore her brother's sight, and in *Edward* the grief and prayers of Matilda, a successful businesswoman, leads to the cure of a female employee.[88] Other unnamed women appear as authorities, petitioners, and friends, as when Ninian 'turned aside to a certain honorable matron's house where he might

[83] Gen Angl 10; CF 56:88.
[84] Gen Angl 18; CF 56:104.
[85] Gen Angl 10; CF 56:88.
[86] Vita E 1.8; CF 56:147.
[87] Gen Angl 10; CF 56:87. Freeman notes that this regendering of Æthelflæd is a medieval convention for powerful women (*Narratives* 76–77).
[88] Vita N 10; Vita E 2.38; CF 56:231.

rest that night'.[89] This casual mention of a woman intimate of the saint recalls Aelred's similar mentions of Mary and Martha of Bethany as friends of Jesus, at whose house he could feed and be fed.[90]

Aelred's inclusion of women in his works has been frequently overlooked, perhaps because he himself calls so little attention to it. Without apology or drama he praises women in the highest social ranks for their virtue, their strength, and their concern to build up the Church and the kingdom, and he shows ordinary english women receiving God's blessing through his saints. His women are remarkable for their virtue, faith, and social or domestic roles rather than for their sex. Aelred recognizes not only kings and saints as models of human virtue and faith but all sorts and conditions of women as well. As he declares that God created men and women as equals, he portrays them as equally sinners and lovers of God, equally recipients and ministers of God's loving-kindness to his creation.

The Manuscripts and Translations of the Historical Works

As far as can be determined from manuscript evidence, *Ninian*, *Hexham*, and *Miracle* were among the least known of Aelred's seven historical works. In comparison to the thirty manuscripts containing *Edward*, only four manuscripts of *Hexham* and three of *Ninian* survive, and *Miracle* is in only one, Cambridge ms Corpus Christi College 139. A nearly complete list of these manuscripts, all but a few in english libraries, appears in Anselm Hoste's 1962 *Bibliographica Aelrediana*.[91]

None of Aelred's seven historical works has yet appeared in a critical edition. *Miracle* and *Hexham* were first printed in the seventeenth century and *Ninian* in the eighteenth.[92] In 1652 Roger

---

[89] Vita N 8.

[90] E.g., Asspt 19; CCCM 2A:151; CF 58:263–264. Inst incl 28; CCCM 1:660–661; CF 2:75–76.

[91] *Bibliotheca Aelrediana*, Instrumenta Patristica 2 (The Hague: Nijhoff, 1962).

[92] Bibliographical detail for the editions mentioned here appear in the Bibliography following the Introduction (123–129).

Twysden included *Miracle* among the five aelredian historical works he printed in his *Historiæ Anglicanæ Scriptores X*, and in 1672 Johannes Mabillon printed *Hexham* from Oxford MS Laud Misc. 668. In 1789 Johannes Pinkerton finally printed *Ninian*, also from Laud Misc. 668. All three works appeared again in the nineteenth century. Twysden's five historical works from Aelred, including *Miracle*, appeared in 1855 in J. P. Migne's volume 195 of the Patrologia Latina. In 1864 James Raine re-edited *Hexham*, again from Laud Misc. 668, alongside the histories of Hexham by Richard of Hexham and John of Hexham, but he followed Mabillon's chapter divisions and inserted Mabillon's titles in brackets. In 1874 Alexander Penrose Forbes reprinted *Ninian*, collating Pinkerton's text with one in a British Library manuscript. And in 1889 W. M. Metcalfe included *Ninian* in his reprint of Pinkerton's two volumes of saints' lives, adding the office for the feast of Ninian from the Aberdeen Breviary.

In this volume the translations of both *Ninian* and *Hexham* follow their most recent printed edition—Pinkerton and Raine, respectively—in both cases with some corrections from the manuscripts. *Miracle* is based on my forthcoming critical edition from Cambridge MS Corpus Christi College 139. The chapter divisions of *Ninian* correspond to textual divisions in the manuscripts, and those in *Hexham* follow those inserted by Mabillon. I have provided the divisions in *Miracle*.

Marsha L. Dutton

Ohio University

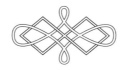

Aelred of Rievaulx
The Lives of the
Northern Saints

THE LIFE OF NINIAN, APOSTLE OF THE SOUTHERN PICTS

PROLOGUE

MANY OF THE WISE MEN who lived before us were zealous to put into writing the lives, practices, and words of the saints, at least of those who flourished in their own times. Their intention was to save from oblivion and perpetuate in memory the example of a more perfect life for the edification of posterity. Those with outstanding abilities and facility in speaking and splendid eloquence succeeded more effectively to the degree that they delighted their hearers with their beautiful speech. Those who lacked the means of speaking with elegance and skill because of the barbarism of their native land did not, however, cheat their posterity of an account of those who were to be imitated, though in a simpler style. So it is that barbarous speech obscured the life of the most holy Ninian, which the sanctity of his way of life and his glorious miracles commend, and the less it pleased readers the less it edified them.

You have been pleased, therefore, my dear friend, to place this burden on me, insignificant though I am, that I should draw the life of this illustrious man out of rustic speech, as if bringing it from a kind of darkness into the light of latin eloquence.[1] That light was indeed set down accurately by earlier writers, but in an extremely barbarous style. I embrace your devotion, I approve your desire, I praise your zeal—but I know my ignorance, and I am afraid that I may strip him of the coarse clothes in which he has until now been concealed without being competent to provide others in which he may appear more resplendent.

But because I cannot refuse what you direct, I will undertake what you demand; I would rather you judged me incompetent than obstinate. Perhaps what my incompetence denies your faith will supply, your prayer will accomplish, your holiness will obtain. He for whose honor and love you ask me to do this will himself be present in your holy prayers, present in your wishes, and present also in my attempt and in my effort. By his merits, furthermore, you are confident that a learned tongue and flowing speech can be given me. You say, moreover, that the clergy and people of your holy church, who hold in extraordinary affection this saint of God under whose patronage they live, will receive whatever we write with the greatest devotion, because, as you assert, the wishes of all have especially chosen me for this work.

I undertake, then, the burden you impose on me, compelled by your prayers but enlivened by faith. I will make the effort, insofar as he who *makes eloquent the tongues of children** deigns to help me. May he so guide my pen that offensive roughness may not too much obscure such great material, nor longwindedness—less eloquent than annoying—cheat the simplicity of those ignorant of rhetorical grandiloquence of the desired fruit of this labor. May the grace of the Saviour, then,

Ws 10:21

---

[1] Aelred's audience is probably a bishop of Whithorn, perhaps Christianus, who was consecrated in 1154. The source and language of the earlier work written in 'an extremely barbarous style' is also unknown; it is unclear whether its 'rustic speech' was Latin or a vernacular language.

assist this undertaking, and may he who conferred on this man the virtues that made him worthy of eternal remembrance also make us worthy who write of them. May he also give us the reward of this labor, so that, during this life by which we are hastening to our homeland, his prayer may always accompany us.* In that departure by which we expect the end of the way and the beginning of life, may we deserve his consolation and, by his holy merits, the eternal reward of the good things of heaven.

* Heb 11:13-16; Augustine, Doc 1.4

PREFACE

Divine authority commends to us the glorious life of the most holy Ninian. That same authority is shown first to have made the holy patriarch Abraham the father of many nations and a prince of the faith, predestined before the ages of the world by an oracle such as this: *'Leave your country, your family, and your father's house and go to the land that I will show you, and I will make you a great nation.'** So it is that blessed Ninian, having left his country and his father's house, learned in a foreign land what afterward he taught in his own. The Lord set him *over nations and kingdoms, to pull down and to destroy, to plant and to build.** Of the sacred beginnings of the most blessed man's way of life and indications of his holiness, the dignity of his office and the fruit of his ministry, his perfect end and the reward of his toil, the Venerable Bede writes in the *Ecclesiastical History* of his people, praising him in very few words:

* Gn 12:1-2

* Jer 1:10

In the year of the Lord's Incarnation 565, at the time when Justin the Younger, succeeding Justinian, assumed the government of the Roman Empire, a priest and abbot named Columba came from Ireland to Britain. He was distinguished by the habit and life of a monk.

He intended to preach the word of God in the provinces of the northern Picts, that is, to those cut off by the high and horrible mountain peaks from their southern regions. The southern Picts themselves, who dwell within these same mountains, had abandoned the error of idolatry much earlier. They had received the true faith when Ninian, a greatly revered bishop and very holy man of the nation of the Britons, preached the word to them. He had been taught the orthodox faith and mysteries of the truth at Rome. The race of the English now holds his episcopal seat, known by the name of the holy Bishop Martin, and the stately church where his body rests along with many saints. This place, which belongs to the province of the Bernicians, is commonly called the White House,* because he built there a church of stone in a way uncommon among the Britons.*

* ad Candidam Casam

* Bede, HE 3.4

What Bede wrote briefly will now, by God's authority, be enlarged upon. From the faithful testimony of this great man we have learned of Ninian's origins. To the fact that he arose from the race of the Britons, Bede adds that he was instructed in the tenets of the faith in the holy Roman Church. We have also learned his office, for Bede commends him as a bishop and preacher of the word of God. We have learned, too, of the fruit of his labor, for Bede asserts that the southern Picts were converted by his diligence from idolatry to the true faith. And we have learned of his end, for Bede declares that he rests with many saints in the church of Saint Martin.

What Bede seems to have touched only briefly, as the character of his history required, the book of Ninian's life and miracles, barbarously written, undertook to enlarge upon for us at greater length. This book, which never deviates from Bede's groundwork, sets down in a historical manner the means by which Ninian made such beginnings, amply deserved such results, and achieved so praiseworthy an end.

BOOK ONE

1. On the island that once, it is said, took the name
Britain from Brutus, among the people of that
name and indeed from no ignoble family, blessed
Ninian took his origin, in that region it is thought
where in the western parts of that island the ocean,
as if stretching out an arm and forming angles on
either side, now divides the kingdoms of the Scots
and the English. Not only by the witness of his-
torians but also by the memories of many others,
that region is known to have had its own king
right up to the most recent period of the English.
Ninian's father was a king, by religion a Christian.
So great were his faith in God and his merits that
he was considered worthy to have a child through
whom what was lacking in the faith of his people
would be supplied and the nation of another
people, who did not know the sacraments of the
faith, would also be imbued with the mysteries of
holy religion.

In his very infancy, having been reborn in the
water of sacred baptism, and clothed in white,
Ninian kept unspotted the white marriage garment
he had received*[2] and, a victor over his vices, pre-   *See Bede, HE 5.7
sented it to the scrutiny of Christ. By his utterly
holy behavior he deserved to have the Holy Spirit,
whom he first received as his purifier, as the en-
lightener within his sacred breast. While he was still
a boy—though he was not boyish in mind—he had,
by the Spirit's teaching, a horror of anything contrary to religious observance, opposed to chastity,
contrary to good habits, or diverging from the laws
of truth. Whatever pertained to the law, to grace,
to honor, or to the good of his neighbor—whatever
was pleasing to God—he never ceased to cultivate
with a mind already mature. Happy was he *whose*

---

[2] At baptism an infant was clothed in a 'chrisom cloth', a white linen cloth
representing its having been washed clean of sin.

* Ps 1:2-3

will was in the law of the Lord day and night, who like
a tree planted by flowing water gave fruit in due season,*
while in manhood he earnestly fulfilled what he
had learned with the greatest devotion. Wonderful was his devotion toward churches and wonderful his love for his companions. He was moderate
in food, sparing in words, assiduous in reading,
pleasing in manners; he abstained from frivolity
and always subjected the flesh to the spirit.

Turning his mind, then, to the sacred Scriptures, once he had learned the tenets of the faith
from some of the more learned men of his people
according to their way, the youth of quick intelligence grasped, according to the meaning he had
received by divine inspiration from the Scriptures,
that they lacked a great deal of perfection. He
began then to be uneasy in mind. Unable to bear
being less than perfect, he grew restless. He sighed.
His *heart, moreover, became hot within him, and as he*

* Ps 39:3 [38:4]

mused a fire was ignited.*

'What shall I do?' he said. 'In my land *I have*
sought him whom my soul loves, and I have not found
him. I will arise, I will go over sea and strand, *I will*

* Sg 3:1-2

seek the truth *that my soul loves.** Is there not a
need for such work? Was it not said to Peter, *"You*
are Peter, and on this rock I will build my church, and

* Mt 16:18

the gates of hell shall not prevail against it"?* Therefore in the faith of Peter there is nothing inferior,
nothing obscure, nothing imperfect, nothing
against which evil doctrine and perverse opinion,
like the gates of hell, can prevail.

'And where is Peter's faith if not in Peter's
see? There certainly, there I must go, so that by
leaving my *country,* my *family, and* my *father's house*
I may deserve to *see the Lord's* will in the land of

* Gn 12:1;
cf. Ps 27 [26]:4

vision and to be sheltered by *his temple.** The de-
ceitful prosperity of this age smiles on me, the
vainglory of the world jests with me, the affection
of my family beguiles me, the hard work and
affliction of the flesh deter me. "But anyone *who*

loves his father or mother more than me", said the Lord,
"*is not worthy of me*", and "Whoever does not *carry
his own cross and follow* me is not worthy of me."*
I have learned too that those despising the royal
court may come to the heavenly kingdom.'

And so, invigorated by a movement of the
Holy Spirit, spurning riches and trampling on all
natural affections, the noble youth determined on
a pilgrimage. He crossed the british sea,[3] entered
Italy through the gallic Alps, and after a successful
journey came at last to the city.[4]

2. Having arrived at Rome, after shedding tears
in token of his devotion before the sacred relics
of the apostles and commending his desire to their
patronage with many prayers, the ever-blessed
young man approached the see of the supreme
bishop. When he had explained to him the reason
for his journey, the pontiff embraced his devotion
and with great affection received him as a son.[5]
He soon gave him over to the teachers of truth
to be imbued with the discipline of faith and the
sound meaning of Scripture.[6]

The young man, filled by God, observed that
he had not exerted himself in vain or to no purpose; he understood that many things contrary to
sound doctrine had been instilled in him and his
fellow countrymen by incompetent teachers.
Then, gasping* with unbounded eagerness for
the Word of God, like a bee he formed for himself
honeycombs of wisdom from the various opinions

* *Lat* inhyans,
*literally 'with his
mouth wide open'*

---

[3] The English Channel

[4] Ninian's pilgrimage to Rome is one of the earliest recorded. On his trip to
Rome in 1140 Aelred probably took this same route through the gallic Alps,
perhaps by way of Susa over Mont Genèvre, by Briançon.

[5] The popes contemporaneous with Saint Martin and so according to this
story most likely to have received Ninian are Damasus I (366–384) and Siricius
(384–399).

[6] On roman schools, see Augustine, Conf 5.8, and Bede, HE 5.7.

of his teachers as from many kinds of flowers.[7] Storing them up in the cell of his breast, he kept them to be pondered and brought out for the refreshment of his interior man and the consolation of many others.*

* Lk 2:19

His recompense was surely worthy, that someone who for the love of truth had spurned his homeland, riches, and revelling was brought, if I may say so, into the very sanctuaries of truth and admitted to the *treasures of wisdom and knowledge.** In exchange for physical goods he received spiritual, for earthly goods heavenly, for temporal goods those that are eternal. Meanwhile, as he was chaste in body, prudent in spirit, farsighted in counsel, and circumspect in his every act and word, everyone spoke well of him, and it so happened that he rose to favor and familiarity with the supreme pontiff himself.

* Col 2:3

When he had sojourned in the city in this praiseworthy way for many years and was sufficiently learned in the sacred Scriptures, he was advanced to the height of virtues, and, borne by the wings of divine love, he was raised up to celestial contemplation. At length, hearing that some in the western part of Britain had not yet received the faith of our Saviour and that some had heard the word of the Gospel either from heretics or from those who knew little of God's law, the roman pontiff was touched by the Spirit of God and consecrated the aforesaid man of God to the episcopate with his own hands. After giving him his blessing, he dispatched him as an apostle to the aforementioned people.

At this time the ever-blessed Martin, bishop of the city of Tours, was still thriving. His Life, glorious in its miracles—which had already been written by the most learned and holy man Sulpi-

---

[7] For this popular medieval image see, e.g., Asser, *Life of Alfred* 76; Aldhem, *On Virginity* (prose) 5–6.

cius—has enlightened the whole world.[8] Returning from the city filled with the Spirit and moved
by desire to see Martin, the man of God turned
his steps toward the city of Tours. Who can easily
say with what joy, what devotion, what affection
Martin received him? By the grace of a prophetic
illumination, the new bishop's virtue was not hidden from him. By God's revelation he recognized
a man sanctified by the Spirit and sure to benefit
the salvation of many.

In the Lord's temple the columns are joined
one to another, and two cherubim, stretching their
wings, touch one another.* Sometimes, borne on
the wings of the virtues, they soar to God; sometimes, standing and lowering their wings, they
become grave with each other. To come back from
higher things to lower, therefore, blessed Ninian
asked that the saint give him masons, saying that
as he had determined to imitate the faith of the holy
Roman Church, he would also imitate its way of
building churches and of establishing ecclesiastical
offices.[9] The most blessed man acceded to his
prayers. And so, nourished by their conversations
together as if by a heavenly banquet, after em-
braces and kisses and tears shed by both, Saint
Martin remained in his own see while Ninian,
with Christ as his guide, hastened to the work to
which the Spirit had sent him.

Once he was back in his own country, there
was a great coming and going of people, great joy
among them all, and wonderful devotion. The
praise of Christ resounded everywhere, for they
held Ninian to be like a prophet. Entering his field
immediately, this assiduous field-worker of the
Lord began *to root out* what was badly planted, *to*

* 1 K 6:23-28;
2 Chr 3:10-13

[8] Saint Martin of Tours (*c.* 316–397); Sulpicius Severus (*c.* 360-*c.* 420) wrote
his *Life of Saint Martin* around 396.

[9] In *c.* 611 Benedict Biscop brought masons to build the monastery of Wearmouth: Bede, *History of the Abbots of Wearmouth* 5.

* Jer 1:10

scatter what was badly gathered, and *to tear down* what was badly built.* And then, when the minds of the faithful had been cleansed of all error, he began to lay the foundations of a sound faith among them, building upon them the gold of wisdom, the silver of knowledge, and the stones of good works.* He taught *by his word* and showed by his *example* everything the faithful were to do,* and he confirmed it by many and great miracles.

* 1 Cor 3:12

* 1 Tm 4:12

3. Ninian chose for his see a place now called Whithorn,* situated on the ocean shore. Extending quite a way into the sea on the east, the west, and the south, it is enclosed by the woven waves themselves; only on the north is there a passageway for those wishing to enter. There, by order of the man of God, the masons whom he had brought with him built a church. Before this, they say, none in Britain had been built of stone. And having now learned that the great Saint Martin, whom he always revered with wonderful affection, had passed over from earth to heaven, he was eager to dedicate this church to his honor.

* Witerna

* Mt 5:15, Mk 4:21

4. And so *the lamp set upon a stand** began to illumine those in the house of God with heavenly signs and the radiant flames of the virtues, to enlighten darkened minds with the lucid and fiery word of the Lord, and to enkindle the indifferent. In that region there was a certain king—for the whole island was divided among various kings—named Tuduvallus. Wealth, power, and repute had excited him to pride, for *the lust of the flesh and the lust of the eyes** and the wealth of the world are incentives to exaltation and pride. As much as a person has, so much does he presume he can have, and so much too does he assume is allowed him. He scorned the warnings of the man of God and secretly disparaged his teaching and his way of life; indeed he resisted his teaching to his face. Thus the land

* 1 Jn 2:16

seemed condemned and near to being cursed; *when it drank in the rain that often fell upon it, it brought forth thorns and thistles** instead of useful grass.

Once when Tuduvallus was being unusually troublesome to the man of God, the heavenly Judge, allowing no further harm to his servant to go unavenged, struck the proud man's head with an unbearable disease; he shattered the hairy pate of the man wandering in his guilty ways. So intense was his suffering that a sudden blindness covered those proud eyes, and he who had attacked the light of truth lost the light of his flesh. The punishment was not in vain, nor was it to mock him. The wretched man lay oppressed by grief and deprived of light, but while he was outwardly in the dark, inwardly he was being enlightened. At last, returning to his heart, he confessed his transgressions, hoping for relief from him alone to whom he had always shown himself an enemy. At last he called his friends and councilors. After he had received their advice, because he was held back by his illness and could not go himself, he sent messengers to the man of God, begging him *not to enter into judgment with his servant** or *to repay him according to his* deeds* but, as an imitator of the Lord's graciousness, to return him *good for evil and love for hatred.**

On hearing this plea the most blessed man was not elated with human vanity. Deeply moved by pity, as always, he prayed to God and then turned to the sick man with the utmost humility and devotion. He first chided the man with a gentle reproach, then touched the sick man's head with his healing hand and impressed on his blind eyes the sign of saving life. What more shall I say? The pain fled, and as light came upon him blindness was put to flight. So it was that the disease of the body cured the disease of the mind, and the power of the man of God expelled the disease of the body. Healed then in both—body and mind,

* Heb 6:7-8; Gn 3:18

* Ps 143 [142]:2
* Ps 103 [102]:10

* Mt 5:43-44; Lk 6:27

that is—Tuduvallus began at last to cherish and revere the holy man of God with complete affection. He knew from experience that *the Lord was with him, directing all his actions** and giving him power over all who raised themselves against the knowledge of Christ, since he was ready to avenge every disobedience and injury inflicted on the servant of Christ.

* Gn 39:23

If then by the grace of humility and penitence this disdainful and haughty man deserved to be thus healed by the holy man, who can doubt that someone who with sure faith and a sincere and *humble heart** asks the help of such a man in healing the wounds of the inner self will obtain a quick remedy through his holy merits? But now let us go on to other things, which seem greater in proportion as they are shown to be contrary to nature.

* Is 57:15

5. In the service of one of the noblemen there was a girl who was lovely in face and beautiful in appearance according to this foul flesh. A shameless youth, having cast his eyes on her, was seized with a blind love. Unable to endure the flame of the lust he had conceived, he began to press the girl to consent to sin. At length he brought about—by prayer or by pay—that she should *conceive sorrow and bring forth iniquity.** The wretched woman was overcome by the other's lust; too little concerned with the judgment of God, she thought she could evade human sight. But her swelling womb revealed her wrongdoing, and soon her *laughter was changed to weeping*, her *joy to sorrow*,* her pleasure to pain.

* Jb 15:35

* Jas 4:9

But what should she do? Where should she turn? She feared the law, her father, and the Lord. So the unhappy woman entered into a pact with death and put her hope in lying. She believed she would appear less guilty if she said she had been deceived or coerced by some man of great name. Driven by the elders to produce the guilty man,

she fixed the crime of debauchery on the priest
to whom the bishop had delegated the care of the
parish. Everyone who heard what she said was
astonished, and they absolved the girl from the
crime that they thought a man of such authority
had committed. The good were scandalized, the
wicked smirked, the common folk snickered, and
the sacred order was blasphemed by the godless.
The priest whose reputation was blighted grieved.
But by the Spirit's revelation the priest's innocence was not concealed from the bishop beloved
of God. Neither did he lightly endure the scandal
to the Church and the harm to holy religion.

Meanwhile *the time came for the woman to be
delivered, and she bore a son**—to the disgrace, not
of the priest, as everyone thought, but of its father
and dishonored mother. For the bishop summoned
every cleric and all the people to the church, and
after preaching them a rousing sermon, he placed
his hand on the candidate for baptism. Meanwhile
the wanton woman, having left all shame behind,
burst in among the crowd with her cronies, thrust
the boy into the face of the priest, and shouted in
the hearing of the entire church that he was the
boy's father, that he had corrupted and deceived
her. An uproar burst out among the people; the
good were ashamed, the wicked amused.

But the holy man, commanding the crowd to
be silent, ordered that the boy, who was only one
night old, be brought to him. Aroused by the
Spirit of God, he looked searchingly at him and
said, 'Alas, my boy. In the name of Jesus Christ, if
this priest begot you, speak out before the people.'
O marvel, worthy of all wonder! O astonishing
mercy of God! O inexpressible power of christian
faith! Truly all things are possible to a believer!

But what shall I say? What could Ninian's
faith not accomplish? Certainly nature yields to
faith and age to power; should not nature yield to
the Lord of nature? Age is not required for agency,

* Lk 2:6-7

nor learning for office, nor time for its exercise. When faith demanded it, divine power *made the tongue of the infant eloquent*, and *out of the mouth of a babe and nursling** he confounded the guilty man, convicted the lying woman, and absolved the innocent priest. From the infant body sounded a manly voice; an untrained tongue formed rational words. Extending his right hand and pointing out his real father among the crowd, he said, 'This is my father! He begot me; he committed the wrongdoing with which the priest is charged. Your priest, O bishop, is innocent of this wicked deed. We have nothing in common except our nature.'

Ws 10:21; Ps 8:2-3 [3]

That was enough. The infant then fell silent, to speak later according to the law of nature and the changes of increasing age. Soon thanksgiving and the voice of praise resounded from everyone's lips, and all the people exulted with joy, understanding that a great prophet had arisen among them and that *God had visited his people.**

Lk 1:68

6. Meanwhile the blessed man took it ill that Zabulus,[10] driven out of the world to beneath the ocean, should have found a haven for himself in a corner of this island, in the hearts of the Picts. For overthrowing his tyranny, the vigorous champion girded himself, taking *the shield of faith, the helmet of salvation, the breastplate* of charity, *and the sword of the Spirit, which is the word of God.** Protected by arms such as these and supported by the company of his holy brothers as by the heavenly host, he invaded the realm of that armed strong man, to rescue from his domination innumerable victims of captivity.

Eph 6:14, 16-17

Approaching the southern Picts, whom pagan error, which still clung to them, compelled to

---

[10] The devil, perhaps from *diabolus*; see Aelred, Inst incl 31.

venerate and worship deaf and dumb idols, he preached the Gospel of truth and the purity of christian faith. The Lord worked with him and *confirmed his message with the following signs*:* the blind see, *the lame walk, lepers are cleansed, the deaf hear, the dead are raised*,* and those oppressed by a demon are set free. He made a gateway for the word of God, and by the grace of the Holy Spirit faith is received, error is renounced, temples are demolished, and churches are built. Rich and poor, *young men and maidens, the old with the young*,* and mothers with their babes[11] hasten to the font of the saving bath; renouncing *Satan and all his works and pomps*,* they are joined to the crowd of believers by faith, by voice, and by the sacraments. They give thanks to the ever-merciful God who has revealed his name in the islands that are far off,* sending them a preacher of truth and the light of their salvation,* and *calling 'his people' those who were not his people, calling 'beloved' her who was not beloved, and calling her who had not received mercy 'one who has received mercy'*.*

> * Mk 16:20
>
> * Lk 7:21-22
>
> * Ps 148:12
>
> * Baptismal renunciations
>
> * Is 5:26
> * Ps 27 [26]:1
>
> * Rom 9:25-26; Hos 1:10

The holy pontiff then began to ordain priests, to consecrate bishops, to distribute the other honors of the ecclesiastical ranks, and to divide the whole land into fixed parishes. Finally, when the children he had begotten in Christ were confirmed in faith and good works, and everything that seemed necessary to the honor of God and the salvation of souls had been arranged, he said farewell to his brothers and returned to his own church. There in perfect tranquility he passed a life perfect in utter holiness and glorious in miracles.

7. It happened on a certain day that the blessed man entered the refectory to take a meal with the brothers. Seeing neither vegetables nor herbs on

---

[11] Cf. Aelred, SS Hag 2.

the tables, he called the brother to whom the care of the garden had been committed and asked why it was that no leeks or herbs had been set out for the brothers that day. He said, 'Truly, Father, any extra leeks or things of that kind I have today committed to the earth, and the garden has not yet produced anything fit to eat.' Then the holy man said, 'Go, and whatever your hand finds, pick it and bring to me.'

Astonished, he stood trembling, hesitating as to what he should do. Knowing, however, that Ninian could order nothing without purpose, he hesitantly entered the garden. An amazing thing, believable only to those who trust that everything is possible to a person of faith! He saw leeks and other kinds of herbs not only growing but even producing seed! He was amazed, and as if caught up in ecstasy he thought he was seeing a vision. Coming to himself, however, and recalling to mind the power of the holy man, he gave thanks to God. When he had gathered what seemed enough, he put it on the table before the pontiff. The guests looked at each other, and with heart and voice together they praised God at work in *[Ps 67:36]*   his saints.* And so they went out, fed much better in spirit than in body.

8. It once pleased the most holy Ninian to visit his dairy herds and the huts of his shepherds. He wanted his flocks, which he had accumulated for the benefit of the brothers, the poor, and pilgrims, to share in his episcopal blessing. And so the animals were gathered in a single place. When the servant of the Lord had looked them over, with raised hands he commended himself and all he had to the divine protection. Walking around them all, he enclosed the cattle by drawing a sort of moderate-sized furrow around them with the staff on which he leaned, ordering that everything within that circle should be under divine protection that

night. This done, the man of God turned aside to a certain honorable matron's house where he might rest that night.

But when, after restoring their bodies with food and their minds with God's word, all of them had given themselves to sleep, thieves crept up. Seeing that the cattle were not shut up in a fold or protected by a hedge or surrounded by a wall, they looked around to see whether guards were present, or anything else that could block their attempt. When they saw that everything was silent and there was nothing to raise the alarm by voice or movement or barking, they crossed the boundaries the saint had fixed and launched their attack on the cattle, struggling to lead them away.

But a divine force was there resisting the ungodly—indeed overwhelming the ungodly. Against those who, like brute animals, considered not their minds but their bellies, it employed a brute beast as its instrument. A bull of the herd, as if roused to fury, charged the men. Attacking the robber chief along with the others, it laid the wretch low and gored his stomach with its horns, spilling his soul along with his entrails. Then, pawing the earth with its hoofs, its foot with astounding force struck a stone it found there. In a marvelous way—as testimony to so great a miracle—its foot sank into the stone as if into soft wax. Leaving its footprint in the rock, by its footprint it gave the place its name. To this day, that place is called in English *Farres Last,*[12] in Latin *Footprint of the Bull.**

* Tauri Vestigium

Meanwhile the ever-blessed father left the appointed place of solemn prayer. Seeing a man

---

[12] *Farres Last* is Old English, from *fearr* 'bull' and *last* 'footprint'. Aelred's identification of the name as English indicates that the story originated in an English-speaking rather than a Celtic-speaking area; it may also indicate that his 'barbarously written' source was in English rather than Latin and that its author gave the place name in English.

disemboweled and lying dead at the feet of the
cattle and the other men scattering, driven by
some kind of frenzy, he was moved with pity.
Turning wholly to God, he begged him to revive
the dead man. He *did not cease from tears** and
prayers until the same power that had killed the
man had restored him, not only alive but also
whole and unharmed. Truly Christ's power struck
him down and healed him on account of that holy
man's merit, *put him to death and revived him, led
him down to the depths and led him back again.**

Meanwhile the other men, whom a kind of
madness had trapped within the enclosure that
the father had drawn, had been running around
all night. Seeing the servant of God, they fell at
his knees in fear and trembling, begging for mercy.
He rebuked them kindly and, by his saving words
teaching them the fear of God and the punishment
prepared for marauders, at length gave them his
blessing and granted them permission to depart.

9. When I ponder the most holy life of the most
holy man, I am ashamed of our own sluggishness,
I am ashamed of the sloth of this wretched gen-
eration. Which of us, I ask, does not often utter,
even if only in our own households, wisecracks
as well as wisdom, words idle as well as useful,
carnal as well as spiritual, during mutual discourse
and conversation? The lips that divine grace has
consecrated for the praise of God and for the
celebration of the sacred mysteries are daily pol-
luted by slander and worldly speech. They weary
of the psalms of God, of the gospel, and of the
prophets; they chatter all day long of people's vain
and shameful works.

What do people do when they travel? Is not
the mind, like the body, in motion all day long,
and the tongue idle? The rumors and deeds of
godless men are rolled in their mouths; religious
gravity is dissipated in laughter and story-telling;

* *Acts 20:31*

* *1 Sm 2:6*

the affairs of kings, the duties of bishops, the min-
istries of clerics, the quarrels of princes, and, above
all, the lives and habits of everyone are talked over.
We pass judgment on everything except our own
judgment, and, what is worse still, we bite *and
devour each other*, so that we *are consumed by each
other*.* * Gal 5:15

Not so the most blessed Ninian. A crowd did
not disturb his quiet or a journey hinder his meditation; nor did his prayer grow lukewarm through
weariness. Wherever he went he raised his mind
to heavenly things either in prayer or contemplation. In truth, as often as he turned aside from his
journey, giving rest to his body and indeed to the
beast he rode on, he brought out a little book that
he carried around for this purpose and took pleasure in reading something or chanting psalms. For
he felt what the prophet said: 'How sweet are your
words *on my tongue, sweeter than honey in my mouth*.'* * Ps 119 [118]:103
For this reason divine power conferred such grace
on him that even when he was lying out under
the sky and reading in the heaviest rain, no moisture ever touched the codex on which he was
concentrating. While the rushing water soaked
every place around him, he sat beneath the water,
alone with his little book as if under the peak of
some roof.

It happened once that this most revered man
took a journey with his brother, an equally holy
man named Plebia. As was his custom, he light-
ened the burden of the journey with the hymns
of David. Some distance along their way, they
turned aside from the public road to rest a bit and
opened their psalters to refresh their spirits with
holy reading. Soon the pleasant tranquility of the
air was overtaken by dark clouds and sent down
the rain water it had drunk in naturally. What
then? The thin air curved like a vault over the
servants of God, as if it were a kind of wall that
remained impenetrable under the downpour.

As they were saying the psalms, blessed Ninian took his eyes off the little book, struck momentarily by a forbidden thought, and was even tickled by some desire at the suggestion of the devil. At once the rain, drenching him and the book, made known what was hidden. Then the brother who was sitting with him, understanding what was happening, reminded him with a gentle reproof of his order and his age and showed him how unbecoming such things were. At once the man of God returned to himself and blushed that he had been overtaken by an idle thought. In the same moment he put aside the thought and stopped the rain.

10. Meanwhile many people—noble as well as middle class—handed over their sons to the blessed bishop to be educated in sacred letters. These he taught by his knowledge and formed by his way of life; by wholesome discipline he drove out the faults that are usually found at that age and instilled the virtues by which they might live humbly, justly, and devoutly.

At one time one of the young men committed a fault that could not be hidden from God's holy man. And because no sinner should go undisciplined, switches—the severest torment of boys— were made ready. The frightened lad fled, but not ignorant of the man's power, he was careful to take with him the staff on which the man was accustomed to lean. He thought that he was acquiring a matchless comfort for his journey by taking with him something belonging to the saint. And so, fleeing the man's presence, he looked for a boat to take him to Scotland.

It is the custom in those regions to weave branches into a vessel in the form of a bowl, of a size that can hold three men sitting close to each other.* Cowhide stretched over it makes it not only buoyant but also impenetrable by water. Pos-

* *a coracle*

sibly ships of immense size were made in that way at that time. The lad stumbled on one of these, as yet uncovered with hide, lying on the shore. When he had incautiously got into it—by divine providence or its own lightness (I know not which, for at a light touch such boats float far on the waves)— the boat was carried out to sea. As the water poured into it, the wretched sailor stood there, not knowing what he should do, where he should turn, or what action was needed. If he deserted the boat his life was in danger; certain death awaited him if he stayed there.

Then indeed the wretched lad, regretting his flight, stared with ashen face at the waves avenging the wrong done to the father. At length, coming to himself and thinking that Saint Ninian was present in his staff, he confessed his guilt with tearful voice as if he were at his feet, asked pardon, and prayed that through the saint's most holy merits divine help might be with him. Then, entrusting himself to the well-known kindness of the bishop as well as to his power, he stuck the staff into one of the holes so that what Ninian could do, even at sea, would not be hidden from posterity. At once, at the touch of the staff, the element became terrified, and as if repelled by divine power it dared no longer seep in through the open holes.

Yours are these deeds, O Christ! Speaking to your disciples you gave your faithful people this promise: *Whoever believes in me will also do the works that I do.** You impressed your sacred footsteps on the waves of the sea; Ninian's power suppressed the natural power of the sea. Your holy hand raised the faltering disciple who was thereby in danger from the waves, lest he be submerged; Ninian's staff protected the fleeing disciple lest he be swallowed up in the billows. You commanded the sea and the winds to dispel your disciples' fear; Ninian's power restrained the winds and the sea

* Jn 14:12

* Mt 14:22-32

so that the lad might reach the shore he longed
for.*

A wind rising in the east impelled the little
boat with a gentle motion. The staff took the wind
like a sail; the staff directed the ship like a rudder;
the staff held the ship like an anchor. People standing on the western shore[13] watched the little boat
resting on the waves like a little bird, not driven
by sails or pushed forward by oars or directed by
a rudder. Astonished, they waited to see what this
miracle might be.

Meanwhile the lad landed. So that the merits
of the man of God might be broadly recognized,
he, animated by faith, planted the staff on the
shore. He asked God that in witness to so great a
miracle it should put down roots and, having
(contrary to nature) taken in moisture, produce
branches and leaves and bring forth flowers and
fruit. Divinity was favorable to his sentiments as
he prayed. At once the dry wood, having sent out
roots and clothed itself in new bark, produced
leaves and branches. Growing afterward into no
ordinary tree, it even now reveals Ninian's power
to all who see it. Miracle is added to miracle! A
crystal-clear spring bursting forth at the root of
the tree emits a shimmering rivulet that winds
along with a gentle murmur, pleasant to look at
and sweet to drink and, because of the merits of
the saint, useful and healthful to the infirm.

11. Ever-blessed Ninian, wonderfully radiant with
these and similar miracles and powerful with the
loftiest virtues, came by a happy course to the day
of his summoning. That day was a day of exultation and joy for the blessed man, but for the
people over whom he had presided a day of trib-
ulation and wretchedness. He exulted because

[13] Manuscripts differ, some having 'western' (*occidentali*), others 'eastern' (*orien-
tali*).

heaven was opening to him; the people grieved because they were being deprived of so great a father. He exulted because an eternal crown was being prepared for him; they grieved because their salvation was being endangered. But his deep affection for them broke in upon his joy, since to desert them seemed painful, but to be separated any longer from Christ seemed intolerable.*   * *Phil 1:22-24*

As his soul wavered thus, Christ consoled him, saying, '*Arise, hasten, my beloved*, my dove, *and come. Arise, my beloved*', he said, 'arise, my dove;* arise   * *Sg 2:10; Sg 5:2* by your understanding, hasten onward by your desire, come by your steadfast love.' These words were clearly appropriate to the blessed man, as he was *the bridegroom's friend** to whom the heavenly   * *Jn 3:29* bridegroom had entrusted his bride, to whom he had revealed his secrets, to whom he had opened his treasures.* Rightly was that soul called *beloved*,   * *Col 2:3;* as everything depended on love, nothing on fear.[14]   [*Is 24:16*] '*My beloved*', he said, '*my dove*'. O dove! a dove taught to moan, who, ignorant of the bitterness of gall, wept with those who were weeping, was weak with the weak, and burned with indignation   * *Rom 12:15;* with those who were cast low.*[15]   *2 Cor 11:29; RB 2.30*

Arise, hasten, my beloved, my dove, *and come; for*   * *Sg 2:10-11;* *the winter is past, the rain is over and gone.** Then   *Sg 5:2* surely, blessed man, the winter was passing for you, because you were made worthy to contemplate with joyful eye the heavenly country that the sun of righteousness illumines with the light of its splendor,* that love inflames, that a wonderful   * *Mal 4:2* spring-like calm tempers with an inexpressible unity of seasons. Then did the wintry storm which disturbs all these earthly things, which hardens the cold hearts of mortal beings with in-rushing vices, and in which truth does not shine fully nor charity burn, pass and disappear forever; then did that

---

[14] Cf. Aelred, Mira 2.
[15] Cf. Aelred, Orat past 7 and Lam D 2.

holy soul in perfect triumph escape from the rain of temptation and the hail of persecution to the glory of perpetual freshness.

* Sg 2:12

Flowers, we read, *have appeared in our land.** The heavenly aroma of the flowers of paradise blew upon you, blessed Ninian, when a flock clad in purple and white smiled peacefully on you as if you were a familiar friend, and into their company they invited you, whom truly chastity has made white and charity made rose. For although the physical death of this martyr did not exhibit the sign without which there is no martyrdom, he was not denied the honor of martyrdom.[16] How often did he present himself to the swords of the wicked, how often did he expose himself for the sake of justice to the weapons of tyrants, ready to lay down his life for the sake of truth, to die for justice! Deservedly then is this man, clad in purple and white, welcomed among the flowers of the roses and the lilies of the valley, as he ascends from Lebanon to be crowned among the

* Sg 4:8

heavenly host.*[17]

* Sg 2:12; Sg 5:2

*For the time of pruning has come.** Like a ripened cluster, Ninian was now to be cut from the branch of the body and from the vineyard of this earthly church, to be pressed by charity and laid up in the

* Sg 2:4; Jn 15:1-5

heavenly storehouses.* The blessed Ninian, perfect in life and mature in age, therefore passed happily from the world and was borne to heaven, with angelic spirits accompanying him, to receive an eternal reward.[18] There, surely, associated with the apostolic choir and added to the ranks of martyrs, enlisted in the host of holy confessors and

[16] In this sentence Aelred may be playing with the two senses of the word *martyr*, both the sense of being put to death for one's faith and its etymological sense of 'witness'.

[17] Traditionally the roses represent martyrdom and the lilies virginity; cf. Ambrose, *Commentarius in Cantica Canticorum* 2.3; PL 15:1874: '*ibi . . . lilia virginum, rosæ martyrum sunt*'. See also Cyprian of Carthage, *Ep* 8; PL 4:249C.

[18] The day of Ninian's death is traditionally given as 16 September.

adorned with virginal garlands, he does not cease
to sustain those who hope in him, who cry out
to him, who praise him.

He was buried in the church of blessed Martin,
which he himself had raised from its foundations.
He was placed in a stone sarcophagus next to the
altar as the clergy and people stood by, celestial
hymns on their lips and sighs and tears in their
hearts. The power that shone in him while he was
alive continues to radiate around the body of the
dead man, so that any person of faith may be
aware that he is alive in heaven who is manifestly
working on earth. At his most sacred tomb the
infirm are cured, lepers are cleansed, the wicked
are cast into fear, and the blind are enlightened:
by all of these the faith of believers is strengthened
to the praise and glory of our Lord Jesus Christ,
who lives and reigns with God the Father in the
unity of the Holy Spirit, for ever and ever. Amen.

BOOK TWO

12. When the ever-blessed Ninian had been transported to the heights, the faithful folk who had
loved him in life often went with great devotion
to what seemed to them to be left of him, namely,
his most holy relics. Divinity, looking favorably
on their devotion and faith, proved by frequent
miracles that his holy one, whom the common
lot had taken from earth, was living in heaven.

A certain man among the folk had a pitiable
son, born of his own wife. He was a sorrow to
both of his parents, a source of astonishment to
the people, and a horror to those who looked at
him. Nature had formed him contrary to nature,
with all his members turned awry. The joints of
his feet were turned backward, his heels were
extended forward, his back met his face while his
chest was near the back of his head, and his arms

were twisted so that his hands touched his elbows.
What more shall I say? This pathetic figure, who
had been given useless members and a fruitless
life, simply lay there. With all his other limbs useless, his tongue alone remained; with it he bewailed his wretchedness and moved those who
saw him to grief and those who heard him to
tears. He was an unremitting sorrow to his parents,
whose sadness increased daily.

At length there came into their minds the
most holy Ninian's majesty, which they had quite
often experienced. Full of faith, they took up that
wretched body. Approaching the relics of the holy
man, they offered *the sacrifice of a contrite heart**
with floods of tears, and they persisted in their
prayers faithfully until evening. Then, laying that
disfigured carcass in front of the saint's tomb, they
said, 'Accept what we offer, O blessed Ninian;
a loathsome gift indeed, but one well suited to
proving your power. We who are feeble, we who
are fatigued, we who are afflicted with sorrow, we
who are overcome with anguish present this to
your loving-kindness. If it is a gift, surely grace is
due us who offer it; if it is a burden, you who have
greater power to relieve it are more capable of
bearing it. Here, then, let him die or live, let him
be healed or perish.' These words, or some like
them, they accompanied with tears, and leaving
the sick boy before the sacred relics they departed.

And behold, in the stillness of the dead of night,
the wretched boy saw a man coming towards him,
shining with a heavenly light and resplendent with
episcopal insignia. Touching his head, this man
ordered him to stand up whole and to give thanks
to God, his healer. When he had departed, the poor
boy awoke as if from a deep sleep. With an easy
movement he twisted each limb into its natural
place, and when he had restored them all, he went
back to his home whole and unharmed. After this

* Ps 51 [50]:19

he gave himself wholly to the church and to ecclesiastical discipline. First tonsured as a cleric and afterward ordained a priest, he finished his life in the service of this father.

13. Once the fame of the miracle had spread, many came running there, pouring out their troubles before the sacred relics. Among them arrived a certain honest man, poor indeed in property but rich in faith and good will. An unusual scabies had invaded his whole body and settled on all his members, so that his skin, strangely hardening, had closed his veins and contracted the arteries everywhere. Nothing but death awaited the suffering man.

The wretched man approached the body of the saint and offered extremely devout prayers to the altar, to faith, and to the Lord. Tears streamed down, sobs erupted, he beat his breast, his very entrails convulsed. The merit of the saint did not fail such faith and contrition, nor did Christ's loving-kindness fail, but both glorified his saint and mercifully saved the wretched man. Why should I delay longer? Poor Edilfrid—for that was his name—did not stop praying until, a few days later, his former health was restored.

14. There was at that time, moreover, a blind girl among the people, Deisuit by name. She was so troubled by an eye ailment that the violence of the disease took away her whole sense of sight. As darkness overcame everything, it hid from her even the light of the sun. This blindness brought grief to the sufferer and sadness to the adults who suffered with her. But what could they do? The skill of the doctors turned into despair, and they sought Ninian, their only hope. Led by the hand before the most holy churchyard, she was left there grieving and sobbing. She sought intently, she asked earnestly, she knocked resolutely. Our loving

Jesus did not deprive her of what he promised in his gospel: *Ask, and you will receive; seek, and you will find; knock, and it will be opened to you.** And so the grace she sought appeared to the aforementioned girl; the door of loving-kindness on which she knocked was opened; the health she asked for was given. When the darkness had been lifted, the lost light was restored. All grief left her. She who had come to the sacred tomb led by another returned to her home led by her own light, to the great joy of her parents.

* *Mt 7:7*

15. Again, two lepers were seen coming into the city. Thinking it presumptuous to touch holy things with a leprous infection, they asked the father's help as if from a distance. Coming to the spring and considering whatever Ninian had touched to be holy, they thought they should wash in that water. A new miracle of the prophet Elisha! A new cleansing, not of one but of two Naamans!* Naaman came in a spirit of presumption, they in a spirit of humility; he in doubt, they in faith. The king of Syria doubted, the king of Israel doubted, Naaman doubted. The king of Syria doubted, he doubted and was arrogant, thinking he should send his leprous servant not to a prophet but to a king. The king of Israel doubted, tearing his clothes at hearing the letter of the king of Syria and saying, 'Am I God, that I can make alive and destroy?' Naaman doubted, going away indignant after hearing the prophet's counsel. Naaman stood in the chariot of pride at Elisha's door.

* *2 K 5*

These men cried out in faith and humility to the mercy of Ninian. Appropriately, his spring was turned into a Jordan and Ninian into a prophet! The lepers were cleansed at the touch of the water but by Ninian's merits, and their flesh was restored like the flesh of a child. They returned to their homes healed, to the glory of Ninian, to the praise of God working wonderfully in his saints.*

* *[Ps 67:36]*

But let there now be an end of this work, although there is as yet no end of the miracles of Saint Ninian. These do not cease to shine forth even in our own day, to the praise and glory of our Lord Jesus Christ, who with the Father and the Holy Spirit lives and reigns for ever and ever. Amen.

THE SAINTS OF THE
CHURCH OF HEXHAM
AND THEIR MIRACLES

Prologue

TODAY'S VENERABLE FESTIVAL, dearest brothers, we must undertake to observe with devotion and celebrate with solemnity in proportion as in it our consolation, our hope, and above all our honor are especially commended. This festival is ours, especially for us who live in this very holy place under the patronage of those in whose honor we have dedicated the joys of this day. It is certainly fitting that we should be zealous at all times to praise them by voice and heart, by act and attachment, but most of all on this principal day of overflowing happiness let us offer the bull-calves of our lips, that is, let us consecrate the very richest sacrifice of praise to the Lord.*

* *Hos 14:2*

Today our experience has verified the presence of the holy relics that our faith has so long maintained; our sight has examined them, our hands have handled them, and our hearts have tasted a draught of interior sweetness.[1] The prophet's

---

[1] The saints celebrated in this work are the five bishops of Hexham buried in Saint Andrew's church there: Eata (678–681, 684–685), Acca (709–733), Frethbert (734–767), Alchmund (767–781), and Tilbert (781–789). In some cases Aelred's dates differ from those given here. Their relics were exhumed and translated to new tombs within the church on 11 March 1155.

* Ps 112:6 [111:7]

opinion is indeed true: *the just will be remembered forever.** From their resting place even their dead bones burgeon with frequent miracles and by clear signs continue to perpetuate their memory, which time had hidden or neglect destroyed. And so it is that our holy fathers, the presence of whose relics we boast, never cease to heap new miracles on old, so as always to increase the devotion of those serving here, to assure their hope, to nourish their love, and by the sight of present gifts to confirm their expectation of future ones. We know that the eyes of some, shut by the night of blindness, obtained the gift of this present light by their merits, that the lame received back the use of their feet, that those in hardship felt the immediate relief of divine consolation, and that at the moment of death those destined for punishment experienced the effect of their prayers in a sudden reprieve. There is a value to bringing forward a few of these things to honor those whose solemn feast we are celebrating, so that from physical, temporal, and earthly benefits we may be led to hope for those that are spiritual, eternal, and heavenly.

When we hear, dearest brothers, that by their prayers these saints restored lost light to the blind, if perhaps a cloud of foolishness has darkened the eyes of our mind, let us fly to them fearlessly for help. Then, with their holy merits revealed and our blindness removed, we may drink in the true light of wisdom. Thus when our spiritual enemies attack us, pelting the wall of virtue with the missiles of temptation, brandishing the fear of endless death, we may know how to destroy them, recalling how powerfully they once snatched a helpless people, besieged in this church, out of the hand of those more powerful and rescued the poor and needy from their despoilers, and how that spiritual attack will be relieved if only we cry out to them in *a spirit of humility and with a contrite heart.** If we

* Is 57:15

are driven to vice by stings of the flesh or goads
of anger, no despair will mute the voice of devout
prayer. We know that, once called upon, the same
loving-kindness that seized a man condemned to
death out of the hand of his attacker will also seize
us who are already engulfed in sin, if we approach
with tears and prayers.

It is evident that the sacred church of Hexham,
founded under the very earliest kings, has long
been resplendent with the dignity of the seat of a
bishop. Always abounding in excellent brethren,
Hexham was an object of terror even to the
powerful men of this world. The ever-blessed
bishop Wilfrid, bringing with him artifacts from
across the seas, renewed it with wonderful stone
work—as you see before you—and beautified it
throughout with pictures and engravings to en-
courage the devotion of an as-yet-uncultivated
people.[2] Reputation soon raised it higher and
brought not only neighbors but even foreign
nations to visit its most sacred threshold.

Because the most holy prelate visited this
church more frequently and cared for it more
devotedly than the others over which he presided,
it happened that after his death all of his people
had recourse to him in this church, as if to someone who was alive. They consulted him in all their
needs as if he were present, and in troubles and
distress they did not so much ask for his help as
demand it. The most holy bishop, well disposed
to their devotion and faith, was always present to
those who called on him, generous to those who
asked of him, consoling to the sad, helpful to the
struggling, and supportive to the wretched—to
such an extent that after his bodily presence was

---

[2] Wilfrid (634–709), bishop of York (664–678), bishop of Hexham (*c.* 686–688,
705–709), after the 678 division of the diocese (cf. chapter 15 below, and Bede,
HE 3.25, 5.19). For Wilfrid's decoration of the church, see Symeon, Kings, AD 788,
and Eddius, *Life of Wilfrid* 22.

gone his spiritual grace flowed forth to them the more richly. Hence we rightly believe that he is participating in this very holy festival, as we have so many indications that he is present.

Book One

1. A certain youth, accused by the authorities of theft and robbery in this city, was bound in chains and held for a long time. When there was no one to provide surety and bond for him, he was at length condemned to death and led out to execution.[3] To our common refuge—that is to say, to Saint Wilfrid—and to the other patron saints of this church he flew in the deepest devotion of his heart, because he could not do so in his body. His feet indeed went where he was being dragged, but he turned his eyes toward the church in great contrition of spirit.

At last he came to his place of execution. No small crowd had gathered for the spectacle; encircling the unhappy man like a crown, they urged the executioner to hurry. This fellow stood there, terrifying of face, strong of hand, and cruel of spirit, and, having raised his sword in both hands, he ordered the captive to stretch out his neck and await one blow of his sword. But he, with his eyes slightly raised, looked at the church and said, 'Help me now, Wilfrid, because if you don't now, soon you won't be able to.' Everyone laughed at the simple-mindedness of his words, and not a few made fun of him. The executioner, himself weak with laughter, hesitated to strike, for fear that, with

---

[3] The system of surety or *borh*, fundamental to the anglo-saxon legal system, was essentially an arrangement for mutual insurance against criminal behavior and penalties. Groups of ten to twelve people pledged surety for their members' adherence to customary law; if any member of the group violated the law, the group bore responsibility for any fines incurred by that person.

the downstroke interrupted, weakness might hinder his ability to strike.

During this slight delay two young men, astride very swift horses, raced up. Presenting surety, according to their native custom, they snatched the youth away from death, freed him from his chains, and allowed him to go away free. Although he had named only the most blessed Wilfrid in his hour of death, no one supposed that the other saints who rest in this present church were not co-workers in this miracle, since he had invoked all of them in his heart, hoped in them all, and in respectful trust lifted his eyes to them all.

Let us consider therefore, dearest brothers, the hope we must have when our souls are endangered and we flee to these our ever-holy fathers, of whose aid we must not despair no matter how strong the temptation. If we should be bound by the chains of some wicked habit, be handed over to one of the spiritual judges to be beaten, and experience what Paul described—'I do not do what I want, and *I see in my members another law at war with the law of my mind and leading me captive into that law of sin'**—let us beg the help of these saints with our eyes raised to heaven and our tears falling copiously. We know that they will *take up arms and shields and arise to help* us.* With our enemy put to flight, they will break our chains so that we may freely run on the way of the Lord's commands with our hearts enlarged,* saying to the Lord with the prophet, *'You have broken my chains; I will offer you a sacrifice of praise.'** This miracle became known to so many that the youth's words, proven effective in so great an extremity, became a common adage among all the people.

* *Rom 7:23*

* *Ps 35 [34]:2*

* *Ps 119 [118]:32*

* *Ps 116 [115]: 16-17*

2. At that time Malcolm, king of the Scots, was laying waste to Northumbria with cruel slaughter.[4]

---

[4] Malcolm III Canmore, r. 1058–1093 (cf. Symeon, Kings, AD ?1079).

He always left the church of Hexham at peace because of his reverence for the saints who rested in it. Once, however, when his messengers fell among thieves near the borders of that church and returned to the king robbed and wounded, they put the blame for this atrocity on the innocent people. At hearing this accusation the furious king raged and swore that because of such ingratitude he would utterly destroy the place and its people. What more shall I say? A fierce army was at the king's command, prepared for spoil, primed for slaughter, and prone to shameful deeds; it neither spared when supplicated nor stopped when sated.

The king's wrath was no secret to the people of Hexham. But what could be done? They had no resources for resistance, no refuge for retreat, no relief through alliance with other people. Their one and only hope was the saints' power, which they had so often experienced. They gathered therefore in the church, *young men and maidens, the old with the young,** women with their infants,[5] to be saved by divine power or struck down before the relics of the saints.

* *Ps 148:12*

The king with his mighty troops was already at hand; he had already seized nearby places on the River Tyne and would have vented his cruelty had not the approaching night hindered his crossing over. Yet the priest who was in charge of the church sent some of his clerics to the king with relics, both to expiate the offense with which they were charged and to beg peace for an innocent people. The enraged king called his Galwegians, men more savage than others, and told them in the hearing of the messengers, 'As soon as daylight comes, cross the river and rush them. Let your eye not ignore and do not pity any order, any sex, or any age. What the sword cannot destroy, let fire; allow nothing of them to remain.'

[5] Cf. Aelred, Vita N 6.

Having spoken, he furiously ordered the messengers to go home. As soon as they returned to the church and related what they had heard, a pitiful tumult broke out, a great outcry, weeping and much wailing. Women bared their heads, tore their hair with their own hands, and beat their breasts; uttering dreadful shrieks in anguished voices, they presented a horrible spectacle to the onlookers. Prostrate on the ground, the men, with more moderation, begged the help of the saints. Priests and clergy endeavored to appease the Lord, sometimes with psalms, sometimes with prayers. Some appealed with groans and outcries to Wilfrid, some to Cuthbert,[6] some to Acca, and not a few to Alchmund.

The priest, sound asleep, was deemed worthy to be consoled by the following vision: he thought he went out of the temple enclosure and by way of exploration turned his eyes here and there. And look! Two men appeared. Their splendid clothing, venerable appearance, tonsure, and demeanor showed him that they were bishops. They were on horseback, approaching the church from the south. Coming to where the priest stood, they dismounted from their horses and said, 'Here, good man, look after our animals. When we have made our prayer in the church we will return to you.' He agreed and awaited their return, not without great astonishment.

After a short time when they returned, one of them sighed deeply. 'Alas', he said, 'what is the cause of this sorrow in the church, this wailing, this outcry, this fear, this pitiful spectacle accompanied by deep sighing and bitter tears?' The priest said to him, 'Do not wonder, good father, for all of us have been given over to punishment, sentenced to death, considered *as sheep for the slaughter**

Jer 12:3

by

---

[6] Saint Cuthbert, bishop of Lindisfarne 685–687, whose relics rest in Durham Cathedral.

the king of Scotland. In the hearing of our clerics he commanded his army to destroy this sacred place and its inhabitants without mercy.'

Then the saint, looking at him serenely, said, 'Do not be afraid, and do not dread them, because I am with you all to save you. As I looked, I saw the affliction of those who are in the church, and I heard their moans, and I have come to free them. Now look, when dawn breaks, I will extend my net from the source of the River Tyne to its mouth.* None of them will be able to cross it or bring any evil upon you.' Then the priest said, 'Who are you, most blessed man, who have come to this wretched people with such needed aid?' He answered, 'I am called Wilfrid, and see, here with me is Saint Cuthbert. I brought him with me as I passed Durham, so that we might come at the same time to our brothers who rest in this church and preserve this place and its people.'

* Job 18:8

He finished speaking, and at once sleep, along with the vision, left the priest. Getting up, he commanded silence and gave a heartening sermon to the people. He ordered them to be calm, knowing that the Lord had looked on their humble prayer and had not scorned their petition: 'For our hope in the saints of God', he said, 'will not disappoint us. We live under their wings, their eyes are upon us, and their ears are open to our prayers.'* Having said this, he asked the clergy to continue their psalms and the others their prayers with a livelier hope.

* 1 Pt 3:12;
Ps 34:15 [33:16]

As the priest reflected silently on his vision, however, he tried to understand the parable of the net. He would have interpreted it as the flooding of the nearby river, except that the pleasant calmness of the air at the time refuted this interpretation. What then? Dawn was already bringing the darkness of night to an end. Showing brighter than usual, it put an end to their hope in the consolation they had believed. Then look! A kind of cloud rising out of the west covered the whole bed of the aforesaid river from its source to its mouth. Compressing itself little by little and quickly thickening, it caused such darkness that if anyone had held out the right hand only a little way, that hand would have been absorbed in the darkness and rendered invisible. The Galwegians entered the cloud, and as they ran through some trackless lands they crossed over the western fork along the way that leads to Cumbria. Around evening they found themselves within the borders of their own territory.[7]

The king, waiting for the Galwegians he had sent out as well as for the lifting of the cloud, which filled him with horror, was in doubt as to what he should do. But as the cloud rising higher revealed the light it had been hiding, the river swelled in a sudden flood. For three days it impeded his efforts. Then the king, coming to himself and calling his barons, said, 'What are we doing? Let us withdraw from here, for these houses are holy.' As the terrifying foe withdrew, thanksgiving and the sound of praise resounded in the church of Hexham: tears and more tears, outcries and more outcries. But security replaced fear, and joy sorrow. Solemn masses were afterwards celebrated with great exultation, and every single person went home with joy.

As for us, dearest brothers, whose duty it is to care for souls rather than for bodies and to guard ourselves against *the powers of the air** rather than those of earth, how many times has he, the king of all the children of pride, armed the minions of his wicked strength to endanger our salvation? How often has the dread host of vices rushed in

* *Eph 2:2*

---

[7] Hexham stands on the south bank of the River Tyne, twenty miles west of Newcastle and a mile southeast of the point at which the South Tyne and the North Tyne merge. The North Tyne rises in the Cheviot Hills, the border between England and Scotland. Malcolm's army, traveling west along the north bank of the river, apparently crossed over the North Tyne to the west rather than south into Hexham and kept it on their right until they reached Scotland.

* *Eph 1:18*

* *2 K 6:15-20*

bands upon us? Let us approach with confidence to the protection of these saints, begging with deep sighs that, like Elisha the prophet, they may strike all our enemies with blindness and, when the eyes of our hearts have been opened,* show us that there are more with us than with them.*

No one should ever think that God's precious saints whose relics are retained here would allow others in, as if they were less than adequate, but rather, to confirm the faith of believers, to increase their devotion, and especially to commend the holiness of the place—for all these reasons, the presence not only of the saints who are present here but also of those who seem to be absent was proven by sure signs. But we must also reflect on the devotion and faith of those who in such dire need lifted up their devout hands and sent up faith-filled prayers, not only to those whom they believed present in their relics but also to those who they did not doubt were absent in body but present in spirit.

3. In the neighborhood of this church there was moreover a man of noble birth and great wealth, Aldan by name. He had a great title as well, as the titles of the great men who were then in this land were reckoned. He used to come often to the holy church of Hexham, especially on feast days. It happened, however, that one day he turned aside to a house where a maiden beautiful in face and graceful in appearance lived in the care of her parents. As soon as the man laid his eyes on her he was overcome with lust. He first tested the girl's constancy by his words. When no result followed his proposition, he leapt up in pride, burning first with anger and then with lust, and turned on her in rage. Aroused as if by Furies,[8] he forgot God and

---

[8] Female personifications of vengeance in classical literature, perhaps known to Aelred from Vergil, *Aeneid* 7; see Aelred, Gen Angl 19.

himself; neither reverencing the presence of the saints nor safeguarding his own soul, he violently seized the girl. Having forcibly taken her from her home, as a wolf does a sheep, he bore her off to serve his lust.

There is in the city of Hexham a church in honor of the holy God-bearer.* It is built to the east of a larger church and is divided from that one by a space, so that a courtyard separates them and allows no passage. When the madman, cruelly carrying the prize he had wickedly seized, got as far as being between the two venerated basilicas, the girl's brother, trying to save the place from contempt and himself and his family from derision, came upon him. But the madman, whose blood, name, and rank sent his heart soaring in pride and whose vitals were inflamed by the fire of lust, added murder to defilement. He ran his pursuer through with his spear, turning against the defender of purity the punishment he himself deserved for his impurity.

* Dei genetrix

But soon the avenging wrath of wounded chastity and murder was at hand and forced the proud man to return to himself. Suddenly his hand stiffened around the spear, and to the end of his life it remained withered and contracted in all his fingers. Eventually, bereft of hearing and sight, he ended his wretched life with an even more wretched death.

4. A certain lay brother renounced the world. Following the example of our father Abraham, he withdrew *from his country and his kindred and his father's house** in order fully and perfectly to exchange his riches for poverty, his pleasures for frugality, and his nobility for voluntary subjection. He settled in this southern part of the northern district of England. Abandoning his possessions, which he had in abundance, as well as some very distinguished man's fortune over which he had

* Gn 12:1-5

great control, he subjected himself to the obedience of this monastery. In no time at all, then, because of the requisite tasks at which he sweated —preferring to weary himself at tasks of a more humble type than to be occupied in those of a higher order, because those were less useful—he was living soberly, justly, and devoutly outside the congregation of the brothers, untonsured and bearded. So it came about that everyone called him Bearded Hugh.

It happened one day that this venerable man, along with one of the brothers, was trying to drag a tree of great size that they had felled out of a steep valley to a place of easier access to vehicles. When the weight of the load exceeded the strength of those moving it, the zealous man—not sparing himself, but summoning all his strength and with great energy moving the mass—incurred a rupture in the sack covering his vital organs so big that it opened a gap three fingers wide. Great pain followed, threatening a permanent weakness in the servant of God. Mindful that his infirmity would burden the poverty of the place and deprive it of the fruit of his welcome labor, his heart was torn by a deep inner sadness, his mind was crushed, and his eyes dissolved in tears.

At length he recollected that he had nearby those who by their holy prayers could easily restore his former strength. He was taken into the church, and with *a pure heart and good conscience and unfeigned faith,** before the relics of the saints he sorrowfully expressed his own distress, his brothers' burden, and the church's loss. With great devotion he asked that they take pity on him. The man rose from his prayer healed. Returning to the necessary tasks in the monastery, he no longer found any sign of infirmity in his body. He lived many years longer. He was sparing in his words, temperate in food, and ordinary in dress, diligently caring for the poor, pilgrims, and orphans, and

* 1 Tm 1:5

faithfully and efficiently managing the affairs of
the church that were assigned to him. Once he
had lifted the house out of the poverty that it had
endured since its beginnings, he gave himself to
monastic discipline. After filling the office of
cellarer for a long time, he fell asleep in the Lord,
*in a good old age and full of days.**

* Gn 25:8

These are a few miracles from the many that
we know were performed by all the saints of this
church together. They commend the holiness of
this place, increase the faith of those who live here,
and arouse their devotion. Allowing our minds to
relax for a while, let us pass on from them to
things by which each one's virtue may appear
separately, as we have learned from true report.

5. We will add to the value of our work if we do
not pass over in silence the way in which in this
town of Hexham in our own times the blessed
Godbearer triumphed over a certain very wicked
man.

At the death of King Henry, who had succeeded his brother William, Stephen usurped sov-
ereign power over the English.[9] Then David, king
of the Scots, zealous with zeal for the cause of
King Henry's daughter, to whom he with all the
English had been bound by an oath, took up arms
against Stephen. He assembled an army and devastated Northumbria by slaughter and burning.[10]
He bore so much respect for the church of
Hexham, however, that not only did he allow no
one to touch anything over which he had rights,

---

[9] Henry I succeeded William II Rufus in 1100 and died in 1135, having
provided for his daughter Matilda (d. 1167) to succeed him. Instead her cousin
Stephen (d. 1154) seized the throne. The ensuing twenty-year civil war between
them devastated England. Aelred's statement here of Stephen's usurpation of the
throne contradicts his praise of Stephen in Bello stand 3, CF 56:254, and indicates
that the work dates from after October 1154.

[10] Cf. Aelred, Lam D 1; Bello stand 1, *passim.*

but he also resolved that as many as had been able to flee there bringing something of their own should enjoy his peace. So it was that when the wicked folk of Galwegians were rampaging with unheard-of cruelty, sparing no sex or age, our men, who were with the king, were moved by pity to transport many whom they had snatched from their power to Hexham, as a certain aid to their salvation.

Blessed Wilfrid had once constructed in that town a church in honor of the most blessed Virgin Mary.[11] It was round, with four porches facing the four corners of the world. It had been destroyed during the ravaging of the Danes and repaired by some priest. A thoroughly wicked youth of that abandoned race, sneaking in during this time, tried to take something by stealth, because he could not do so by force. But as all were protecting their possessions, his wicked will bore no fruit.

When eventually the cruel robber came to the church of the most blessed Virgin, he circled it, vainly seeking an entrance. When he found the door barred, he grasped a stone in his sacrilegious hand as if he would break the bar. Up to this point the Virgin bore her affront. At that moment, however, as the people looked on, he was handed over to an extremely evil demon to pay the wholly just penalty for his presumption. The unhappy fellow ran about this way and that, crying out and wailing; he foamed at the mouth and rolled his eyes, now sticking out his tongue, now pulling at it, now barbarously gnashing his teeth; he thrashed his arms in frightful motions and tore his clothes and his flesh with his sacrilegious hands. After he had provided the people with the frightful spectacle of his misfortune for a few days and they could no longer bear such horror, they hauled him out of town, and beside the nearby river they left

---

[11] Cf. chapter 3 above.

him for as long as the evil spirit harried him, until
he should yield his expelled soul to the depths
and give his body to the beasts and birds.

BOOK TWO

6. Let us make a beginning on our account of the
miracles of the saints who rest in the holy church
of Hexham—those deeds that we are going to
make known one by one in this history—with
the holy bishop Acca. He succeeded blessed
Wilfrid in ruling over the holy church at Hexham;
he was Wilfrid's fellow traveler in his pilgrimage,
sharer in his troubles, partner in his exile, and
companion in his solitude. Acca was first formed
as a cleric by the most holy Bosa, the most devout
bishop of York;[12] later he spent a period of time
subject to the teaching of Saint Wilfrid, until the
death of that father. After traveling to Rome, he
thoroughly learned the ecclesiastical precepts and
the canons of the fathers and, faithfully laying
them up in the sacred bookchest of his heart, at
an appropriate place and an opportune time, he
delivered them to those subject to him to observe.

During this journey the aforesaid Wilfrid,
a man of the Lord, spoke of that great revelation
by which divine grace, through the holy archangel
Michael, had promised him a rapid return, a pros-
perous journey, tranquility of life, restoration of
his reputation and possessions, and the exact day
of his demise. He disclosed secrets to blessed Acca
beyond other mortals.[13]

---

[12] Bosa, bishop of York 678–686, 691–705. Bosa, a monk of Whitby (Bede, HE 4.23) and formerly bishop of Deira, replaced Wilfrid at York when he was expelled by Egfrid (Bede, HE 4.12) but was then replaced by the returning Wilfrid, armed with a papal vindication (Eddius, Life 54).

[13] Eddius describes Acca as a man of acute intelligence (Life 56).

Acca's great devotion to God after he had been enthroned, his many kindnesses to his neighbors, his instruction of those subject to him, his punctiliousness concerning the Divine Office, and his attentiveness to the sacred Scriptures you have learned from the testimony of the Venerable Bede, priest. The books that this learned man wrote in response to the requests of such a great bishop, dedicating them to him in their prefaces, are even to this day his witnesses.[14] In them Bede gracefully described Acca's devotion and his skill in divine eloquence.

But why should we seek other witnesses to Acca's holiness when we have at hand what I may call eloquent tokens? We can easily touch them with our hands and see them with our eyes. Divine miracles shine forth from them, and unmistakable traces of his spotless life remain in them, should some unbeliever deny them. Who, I ask you, has preserved safe from all corruption the sacred garments in which his holy relics were wrapped in the earth for three hundred years, if not *God, who is wonderful in his saints*?* To commend the incorruption of his life, God applied the gift of integrity, which his flesh earned in life, to his clothing as he lay in the sepulcher. Surely you possess his silk chasuble and likewise his dalmatic, as well as a linen cloth in which the former beauty is preserved and the original strength endures: their nature has not given way, earth has not harmed them, and their beauty has not departed.

But why, someone may ask, do you ascribe to his clothing, on account of the exceptional merits of his flesh, what we know to have been denied to his flesh? For we found bones, not flesh, rolled up in these clothes in the dust under the earth. But far be it from us to say that this reward was denied

* [Ps 67:36]

---

[14] Bede dedicated several of his late works to Acca.

his flesh. Surely it was not denied but only delayed. Incorruption of the flesh does not pertain to this mortality but to future eternity. In this way is God's saint glorified: in the things of time he will be glorified for a time; in eternal matters he will be glorified eternally, when *his mortal nature will put on immortality and his corruptible nature will put on incorruption.**

* *1 Cor 15:53*

Meanwhile we have in his clothing a mark of his sanctity, a sign of incorruption, the innocence of chastity. Who would not be roused to obtain fleshly purity, knowing it to be acceptable to the Lord, pleasing to the angels, and revered by human beings, recognizing that it is a kind of beauty common to all the virtues, a kind of power that conquers every vice? To it nature yields, at it age is amazed; it imitates eternity and exalts the marks of resurrection. Nor is the gift of healing absent around his most sacred relics, where we know that the blind have been enlightened, the arrogant cast into fear, and the lame cured.

7. There was in a neighboring region a man by the name of Raven, who lived an ordinary life under a certain extremely rich nobleman. He was a man simple and upright, according to his capability, and greatly devoted beyond the other saints to the ever-blessed Acca. Suddenly blindness came upon his eyes and completely took from him the faculty of seeing. For three years, day was turned into night for him. In vain he hoped for a cure from the doctors, but a heavenly medicine was reserved for him. At length the diseased man returned to himself, and recalling his gift of faith and devotion, he asked, 'What am I doing? Where is my common sense? How long will my faith sleep? How long will my devotion cool? Why do I tremble? Why pretend? I will rise; I will rise; I will go to my Acca. Perhaps he will hear and take pity on his humble servant and turn night to day, and after these

* Job 17:11

day-long shadows he will restore the joys of the light for which I long.'*

Now the birthday of the most blessed Acca was at hand, the day on which he passed joyously from this corporeal darkness to the splendor of true light,[15] a day celebrated by the inhabitants of the region with great honor every year. Judging this an opportune time to seek the favor he was hoping for, the man asked to be led to the church. The man fell to prayer, frequently kissed the sacred altar, moistened the ground with his tears, and so passed the greater part of the night sleepless. At length a deep sleep overcame the weary man, and he saw in a vision the saint of the Lord standing near him. The saint's face was shining, he was beautifully clothed, and he bore the pontifical insignia. Delighting the man by his joyful countenance, he said, 'O man, you put great trust in the saints of this church.' And he said, 'Truly, Lord, for Saint Acca the bishop is my sole and special refuge.' The saint said to him, 'And not in vain or by folly. I am Acca, the bishop. You should know that you have been healed by my prayers.'

The man rose, now seeing, and looked around in wonder at those who were watching him. He thought he was seeing a vision. Then, addressing a man who was sitting near him, he asked, 'Isn't that you?' And he answered, 'It is I. Don't you see me?' 'Yes', he said, 'I see, if I'm not still asleep.' He leaped up and proclaimed the miracle publicly. In everyone's mouth were the words 'Raven! Raven sees!' They all rose up and offered a *sacrifice with shouts of joy in the Lord's tabernacle*;* they chanted and sang a hymn. When a report of the miracle was brought to the man's master, he—wishing to gain favor with the saint—gave the man, whom

* Ps 27 [26]:6

[15] The traditional date of Acca's death is 20 October. A weathered plinth now in the south transept of Hexham Abbey church is believed to be all that remains of the cross that once marked Acca's grave.

he freed, and all his own money to the saint and
directed the man to serve this church as long as
he lived.

Would that we, dearest brothers, might in
dangers to our souls implore his aid with the same
faith, equal devotion, and no less hope, mindful of
the tears and the constancy in prayer by which a
man of flesh obtained help for his flesh. You who
are spiritual should offer to such a father libations
of tears against the spiritual weaknesses of your
souls. You should present the sacrifice of your
prayers and ignite with the fire of charity a holo-
caust of vigils and psalms on the altar of your
heart.

8. Nor do I think I should pass over in silence how
a blind woman was healed by the power of the
holy relics.[16] You know, brothers, how two boxes
are reported to have been found under the holy
altar by the venerable man Edric, who in this
church first established the life and practices of
the Regular Canons, according to the form of the
apostolic tradition.[17] According to their inscrip-
tions, one of them held some bones from the
remains of Saint Acca and the other some from
blessed Alchmund, mixed with dust. And lest the
value of the treasure that the devout investigator
had found be hidden from its finder, their efficacy
was confirmed by miracles.

A certain woman, deprived of eyesight but
faithful in spirit, was wearing out the threshold of
the church by day and by night. Because the poor
soul had sometimes to do without the assistance
of a guide, the aforesaid brother, having compassion on her unhappy condition, often gave her his

[16] The stories in chapters 8 and 9 are also in Symeon, Kings, AD 740.
[17] Edric was probably the leader of the first group of augustinian canons to
settle in Hexham before Archbishop Thurstan sent Aschatil to be prior in 1114;
cf. chapter 12 below and Symeon, Kings, AD 1112.

hand and directed her steps. On a certain day, when he offered his usual kind help to her in her need, it occurred to him to test the power of the holy relics he had found. Entering the sacred repository, he prayed, then drew out one of the bones and dipped it in water.

Going to the blind woman, he bade her trust in the merits and power of the holy bishop Acca. She assented and honored the bearer of the holy treasure with bent knee and bowed head. Then he touched her eyes with the healing water, and after signing her with the cross he asked that the power of the most blessed father be present. A miracle! At the touch of the heavenly water some divine power immediately separated her joined eyelids, and as darkness slowly gave way the long-desired light took its place. Both of them rejoiced, she because of bodily benefit, he because he experienced the effect of spiritual fruit.

9. And so the venerable brother, emboldened by this experience and going forward as if from faith to faith, became more certain of the power of the most holy bishop. As often as opportunity offered he asked a gift from the heavenly power. It happened that a craftsman, at that time the only one of that city to give the inhabitants the benefits of his craft, was suffering from an intercutaneous disease of the throat. It was so bad that the size of the swelling prevented him from speaking and blocked the passage by which his food passed down. The city was imperiled; while he feared the loss of his health, everyone else feared the loss of his necessary craft.

But while others despaired, the brother I have often mentioned relied on the remedy of heavenly grace. 'Will not the power that turns darkness into light', he asked, 'easily reduce this swelling?' Thereupon, water into which he had dipped the sacred relics was brought, and he poured it into the suffer-

er's mouth. A miracle! The heavenly stream attacked
the disease. Immediately, as if not water but a knife
had gone in, the skin at the bottom of the swelling
burst and the harmful sanies was expelled. As the
swelling gradually subsided, a way was opened for
his voice and a passage for food. So it happened that
by one and the same miracle health was restored
to a man and an essential craft to the city.

10. In our time two men who had lived as brothers from their boyhood were given their legal
inheritances. Already deemed illustrious because
of their homes, families, and money, they were
dearer still in the esteem of their fellow citizens
by reason of their faith and good lives. They both
agreed to go to see the places of the holy resurrection and of the Lord's passion, so that they
might be worthy of the forgiveness of their sins,
there where the sins of the whole world were
expunged by the blood of Christ. They encouraged each other, and when they had by frequent
discussions arrived at a suitable time, fortified by
the sign of the cross and commending themselves
devoutly to the patronage of the saints and the
prayers of the brothers, they undertook the
longed-for journey.

When they had passed physically over the sea,
pilgrims coming from other regions joined them
to make a single group. Calling on the patron of
their city familiarly day after day, as was their custom, the aforesaid men visited Saint Acca in their
daily prayers, and when in friendly conversation
they mentioned how deserving he was, their companions rejected and mocked their words. A certain
cleric, who with his sister fell into their company,
said that he did not know who that Acca was and
accused the young men of simple-mindedness and
rustic manners. He said that although they called
Acca a saint, he had neither heard of his powers nor
found his name in the catalogue of the fathers.

This most unhappy soul disputed the merits
of the saint according to his own stupidity, thinking that nothing had been written that he had not
read and that no blessed man abounded in virtues
of whom he had not heard. He laughed at the
inexperience of those who in their simplicity revealed their faith by their simple words and who
prayed that the most blessed Acca would be with
them. Adding blasphemy to blasphemy, he became
carried away in laughter at the saint of the Lord.
The young men did not listen to any more from
the abusive man but expressed their indignation
with righteous imprecations. The whole company
disliked the blasphemer; judging him unworthy
of their companionship, they forced him to leave
them. As they advanced toward him, the abusive
man stood still and, suddenly struck down with a
terrible faintness, *fell to the ground and rolled about,*
* Mk 9:20 [19]   *foaming at the mouth.**

The man's pitiable appearance caused his sister
to dissolve in tears. But what should she do? She
was afraid of her companions, whom her brother
had irritated, and doing nothing brought him no
comfort. Her grief drove her to beg assistance
from those to whom he had shown himself possessed of such excessive perversity. Running in
tears after those ahead of her, she loudly bewailed
her misfortune; she begged them to give her some
counsel for him in his peril. They all refused, grati-
fied that the blasphemer had rightly been struck
down.

One of the young men, however, was moved
with pity. 'Do you now believe that Saint Acca is
able to help you in this danger?' he asked. At the
name of the saint the man opened his eyes and,
seeing the young man, he said with as much voice
as he could, 'I believe; I believe; truly and from the
heart, I believe, and I give you the pledge of my
faith: only pray for me.' The young man prayed,
and at almost the same moment that he rose from

his prayer, the other man rose from the ground. Then they put him on an animal, and he came to his companions no longer a blasphemer but a devoted advocate of Acca's sanctity. From then on no one was more fervent in his praise of blessed Acca, no one more sure in faith in his power, no one more certain of his help and consolation when in danger from rivers, in danger from thieves, in danger from mountains.

Having received many benefits from the blessed confessor on their journey and having visited the holy places, the young men returned home successfully, bringing proper gifts to the saint and reporting the miracle to the people.

11. After the devastation of the Northumbrians, which the Danes lamentably brought about on their invasions into England,[18] what happened to the other churches happened also to Hexham. To use the prophet's words, she lay groaning for a long time without a priest, *without ephod or teraphim.* ** Hos 3:4* Then *she wept bitterly in the night, with tears on her cheeks.* * * Lam 1:2* Anything made of wood, fire consumed; the widely renowned library that the holy bishop had founded perished entirely. There can be no doubt that in the devastation the memorials of the lives and miracles of the saints that our holy fathers had transmitted in writing for the instruction of posterity were destroyed.

At last, when the furious persecution cooled and the serenity of peace smiled down, a certain priest graced with many virtues was active in the church of Durham. He was revered in the place of a father by all the northern English, who stood so in awe of his words that whatever they heard from him they accepted as a divine utterance. He

[18] The ninth-century danish invasions of England peaked between 866 and 875, during which time all of England north of the Thames was settled by the Danes and ruled by them. The defeat of Northumbria took place in 875.

was called Alfred, son of Westou, or even, because of his gifts of teaching and wisdom, Alfred Larwa, that is, 'teacher'.[19] Prompted by divine revelation, as he passed through the sacred places laid waste by the savagery of the barbarians, he took the relics of many saints from their burial places and transferred them to the church at Durham. He came to the holy church of Hexham and took up the relics of Saint Acca. But foreseeing (perhaps in spirit, for he is also said to have had the spirit of prophecy) what sacredness and honor this church was to have, he was unwilling, or unable, to take away these sacred relics. He concealed them decently inside the church, taking thought for veneration of places, the devotion of people of his time, and the improvement of those to come, as divine grace directed him.

When Northumbria had somewhat recovered under King Edward[20] and the dispersed relics had been restored to their proper places, the people undertook to build up the ruins. But again in the reign of William, when Walcher the bishop was murdered by the English, desolation and flight from calamity followed.[21] William, in habit a monk, succeeded Walcher.[22] Turning the clerics out of the church at Durham, he replaced them with monks. Certainly he arranged positions outside the church for some, but he did not hesitate to expel others who refused to accept it.

---

[19] Aelred's great grandfather, sacristan of the cathedral of Durham and custodian of the shrine of Saint Cuthbert. Symeon of Durham credits him with bringing the bones of Bede to rest at Durham (Church 3.7).

[20] Edward the Confessor, r. 1042–1066.

[21] Walcher, bishop of Durham 1071–1080, was slain in the church at Gateshead by a mob protesting the abuses that his ecclesial subordinates and his soldiers had carried out against the church and people (Symeon, Church 3.23–24).

[22] After the murder of Walcher, William I named William of Saint Carileph (1081–1096), previously abbot of the Norman abbey of St. Vincent, to the bishopric of Durham (Symeon, Church 4.1–3).

Among these was the son of the aforesaid Alfred, who presided over the others.[23] When he received nothing from the bishop, he went to the venerable Archbishop Thomas who first ruled over the church of the Normans at York, asking that he be allowed to rebuild the church of Hexham.[24] The venerable pontiff agreed to his request and committed to him the aforesaid church to direct. When the man came to the place he found everything desolate, the walls of the roofless church overgrown with grass and overrun by the encroaching forest. Defaced by rain and ravaged by storms, it retained nothing of its former beauty. The land was so desolate that for almost two years he sustained himself and his family only by hunting and fowling. Determined to restore the church, he began at the east end, where he erected an altar and fitted it out properly for the heavenly sacrifice.

But soon after undertaking the work, he departed this life and left the fruit of his labors to his son.[25] He, though a sinner who lived otherwise than he ought to have, showed himself nonetheless devout and careful in restoring, furnishing, and preserving the churches of Christ.

Directing all his attention and care to restoring the Hexham church, he cut down the encroaching forest, cleared the overgrown walls,

---

[23] Eilaf, Aelred's grandfather and treasurer of the church of Durham.

[24] The church of Saint Andrew at Hexham was in the gift of the bishop of Durham until the death of Bishop Æthelwine in 1071, at which time the first Thomas to be archbishop of York (1070–1100) took possession of Hexham. Alfred, son of Westou, had apparently received the benefice of Hexham from Edmund, bishop of Durham (1021–1041), but both he and later his son Eilaf maintained curates there until William expelled married canons—including Eilaf—from their posts at the cathedral. For Eilaf to confirm his right to the church with Thomas as he prepared to move his family from Durham to Hexham would have been a wise precaution.

[25] Another Eilaf, Aelred's father.

roofed the whole church with tiles, and, when the walls had been plastered inside and out, decorated the church with an ancient painting of great beauty. After laying a floor of squared stones in the eastern part, he erected an altar set on columns in an appropriate place. Considering it unfitting that the sacred relics should be buried in a place out of sight, he decided to have them dug up from their burial place with due ceremony and placed more fittingly in an casket covered by a pall, behind the high altar.[26] The bones thus taken from their burial place he set on linen cloths in the southern porch, above the altar of Saint Michael, until everything was ready in the place where they were to be placed.

To guard them he set his younger brother, by name Aldred, afterwards a canon of good life and sound habits in this church, who was trustworthy because of his simplicity. Gazing at the sacred relics there in his presence, the young man, moved by a kind of interior sweetness, longed to possess some small part of them. 'This church alone', he said, 'ought not to glory in such a gift when such a multitude of bones could satisfy many churches.' Reluctant, however, to touch such a shrine with his hand, he recited the seven penitential psalms* with tears and contrition.

Pss 6, 32 [31], 38 [37], 51 [50], 102 [101], 130 [129], 142

When his prayer was completed, he went to the porch. As he entered it, he met with a fire of such heat that he thought he could suffer nothing like it at the mouth of a burning furnace. Terrified, he turned back, believing himself undeserving of so important a charge. He prostrated himself again, he wept, he beat his breast, and, repeating the sacred psalms, he tried to approach. But at once an even fiercer heat came out of the porch, repelling him as he tried to enter; it took from him

[26] Cf. Symeon, Kings, AD 740.

even any hope of entering, for he did not dare to try a third time.

When his brother, who was in charge of the church, heard about this, he broke into tears. With great devotion and compunction, and with due honor, he replaced the most sacred relics— wrapped in a very precious cloth and collected in a suitable chest—on a stone table that he had properly prepared.

As this priest's devotion to the saints increased, he began to reflect more rigorously on his own unworthiness, on the sanctity of the church, and on reverence for the saints. Judging himself unworthy to approach such great fathers, he also feared that after his death the church would be given to others who, even if not less worthy, would certainly be less careful than he. Burning with zeal for the house of God, he went to that venerable man, the younger Thomas, archbishop of York,[27] and humbly asked that he commit the church to the canons regular and that he hand over to them himself and his property. When the venerable prelate had agreed to his request, he built with his own hands some buildings suitable for the religious life, but of wood.[28]

With the approval of the aforesaid pontiff he first brought into the church at Hexham two brothers of virtuous life, one of whom had passed his life laudably in the church at York, the other at Beverley. After the death of Thomas,[29] Thurstan, who succeeded him, committed the care of this church to Aschatil, a canon of the monastery at

[27] Thomas II, archbishop 1109–1114, was the nephew of his predecessor but one, Thomas I of Bayeux.

[28] For a different version of Thomas's sending canons to Hexham, see Richard of Hexham, History 8–9.

[29] Thomas died in 1114, when Aelred was four years old. Walter Daniel recounts Aelred's announcing the death of the archbishop three days before the news reached Hexham (Ep M 2; CF 57:151–52).

Huntingdon, decreeing that the regular life should be observed there forever.[30]

Aschatil was a refined and affable man, taught to conform to the customs of all and to win the favor of rich and poor, of clerics, soldiers, and peasants. During his time he did much for the house of God, in spiritual as well as in temporal matters, so that, in short, he made it teem with good and honorable men professing the regular life. He furnished them with appropriate buildings well constructed of stone and roofed with wooden tile, an enclosure acceptable to the inhabitants. Furthermore, he embellished the church with precious ornaments and enriched it with the relics of Saint Andrew and other saints, increasing the devotion of both visitors and inhabitants.

He was succeeded by a certain observant and highly learned man, Robert, surnamed Biseth, who had been professed in the same church. As he was more suited to religious observance than to the administration of external affairs, after a few years he renounced the pastoral charge.[31] His successor was Richard, from his youth a man of honest and sober life.[32] Even while he was still in the world, he was reckoned almost a monk on account of his manifest chastity and sobriety.

Meanwhile inner devotion grew and love was being greatly roused among the brothers, to whom the power of the saints had so often shone forth. They sensed their presence not only in their relics but also in their miracles, by which they were consoled in times of sadness, directed in times of joy, upheld when they were tempted, defended when they were threatened by persecution, and heeded when they fled to them in any need.[33]

[30] Thurstan, archbishop of York 1119–40 (elected 1114, consecrated 1119).
[31] Robert Biseth (1130–1141) left Hexham to become a monk at Clairvaux.
[32] Richard of Hexham (1142–?1170)
[33] Cf. Aelred, Inst incl 32.

And because the brothers were daily enriched by temporal wealth through the saints' merits, they strove to increase their temporal glory. They considered unworthy of the saints the containers of ordinary wood, which offered nothing of glory and honor to the eyes of those who were so often gladdened by their benefits. First *the hearts of all became warm within them, and, in their meditation, a fire burned.* Then, talking among themselves and frequently discussing these things, they became mutually enflamed and began making more serious inquiries about how they might remedy the situation. At length, brought together over the matter at the prior's instruction, they aroused the devotion of the holy man by their desire.

* Ps 39:3 [38:4]

When they had all agreed, they undertook the desired work. With generous spirits and eager hearts, those responsible furnished what was needed. They prepared a casket of suitable size and covered it with silver and gold. They inserted jewels in appropriate places, and by the craftmen's skill they diversified the work with the highest beauty. They also fabricated two smaller ones of no less beauty, though not of the same value. In the year of the Lord's incarnation 1154, when everything was ready, the prior set the fifth nones of March* as the solemnity on which the relics would be transferred. Meanwhile the brothers prepared themselves for this great task by psalms and prayers and spiritual exercises.

* 3 March

When the appointed day had come, the prior and the brothers assembled in the church around the third hour.* Barefoot, they prostrated themselves before the holy altar. Adding appropriate prayers to the penitential psalms, with resonant voices they chanted the responsory used in the church to honor holy confessors. When the solemn collect after the chant was concluded, the brothers processed in, vested in albs and unshod. At the altar steps they displayed the relics with the receptacle

* Tierce, c. 9 AM

in which they had hitherto been preserved, to be
reverenced, and when the sacred tokens had been
taken from there, they laid them on the floor with
the greatest reverence, a cloth becomingly spread
beneath them.

There were the bones of four saints, separated
one from another and wrapped in extremely
beautiful cloths. As soon as they began to unroll
them, a wonderful fragrance issued forth, striking
the nostrils of all and softening all their hearts.
Astonished at this divine visitation, the brothers
at first thought that the saints had been buried
with spices. But when no sign of that appeared,
they understood that God's saints had bestowed
on their holy relics this gift from the odors of
paradise that they forever enjoy.

Much strengthened by these things, they examined the sacred remains of the first of the saints.
The bones were found to be shimmering with a
heavenly beauty, clearly revealing their holiness by
their color as well as by their fragrance. They thus
drew everyone's attention to themselves and
aroused their emotions, so that no one would
doubt him to be spiritually present whose relics
they perceived to be suffused with so much grace
and so venerable in their dignity.

Lest posterity should have any doubt con-
cerning the name of the holy confessor, the one
who had buried him had removed every scruple
by written testimony. For they found in the wrap-
ping this document: IN THE YEAR OF THE LORD'S
INCARNATION 740, ON THE FOURTEENTH KALENDS
OF NOVEMBER,* BISHOP ACCA OF REVEREND MEMORY
PASSED FROM EARTH TO HEAVEN IN THE TWENTY-
FOURTH YEAR OF HIS EPISCOPATE. HERE MAY HIS
REMAINS REST IN PEACE.

Not yet satisfied, although much revived by
this most sacred vision, they rolled up the heavenly
tokens again in perfectly clean cloths and hid
them away again with due honor. And lest with-

* 20 October

out documentation the saint's name and merits should be lost to the memory of future ages, they wrote them down on vellum and inscribed them on lead plates and affixed them to the relics.

Then they turned to inspect the relics of Saint Alchmund. When they had taken them out with equal glory and honor, they read a document that contained his name and office. The text of this writing was: IN THE YEAR OF OUR LORD 780, ON THE SEVENTH IDES OF SEPTEMBER,* ALCHMUND, BISHOP OF THE CHURCH AT HEXHAM FOR THIRTEEN YEARS, DIED. FOR HIS MERITS HE BECAME A PARTICI-PANT IN ETERNAL BEATITUDE; HERE MAY HE REST IN PEACE.

* 7 September

The brothers stood around the heavenly trea-sure; intently examining everything, they found every part of the human body. And because those who had once buried the saints had taken some bits of the bones of blessed Acca for their devotions, they marveled that no such thing had been done to the remains of blessed Alchmund. Why this had not occurred, some had forgotten and others had not heard. So I am not at all reluctant to add an account of his former translation to his new one and to explain the reason for his integrity.

12. At the time when the priest Alfred, whom I mentioned above, was revered in the place of a father by both leaders and people in all the churches of the Northumbrians, a certain man, a thegn of minor rank, was in possession of the church at Hexham.[34] He was greatly devoted to the patrons of the place, though a simple man, endowed with faith rather than knowledge. One night when his body was asleep, an old man of reverend countenance stood near him in a vision.

---

[34] Perhaps Collan, Alfred's brother-in-law, a descendant of the Lindisfarne monks who carried Saint Cuthbert's body to Durham and one of the provosts responsible for the land held by the bishops of Durham.

He was distinguished by a bishop's insignia and shining with celestial light.

Giving the man a light tap with the pastoral staff he was holding in his hand, as if to rouse him from sleep, he said, 'Go quickly and tell Alfred, the priest of Durham, that when he has gathered the people of Hexham together he must take my body from the tomb, lift it higher, and bury it again in a more honorable place in the church. It is right that people should show honor on earth to those whom Christ has judged worthy of glorification among the angels in heaven.'

The priest was astonished, stunned by the splendor of the light as well as by the authority of the voice. When he had somewhat recovered his spirits, he inquired humbly and reverently who this might be. 'I', said the saint, 'am Alchmund, who was the fourth after blessed Wilfrid to rule the church at Hexham. After *the fight I fought*, after *the race I finished*, after *the faith I kept*, I obtained *the crown of righteousness* through Christ's grace.* I was buried next to my venerable and holy predecessor, Acca. When the aforesaid priest—with your help—searches diligently for my body, he will surely find it.' As he said this he withdrew in his invisible and incomprehensible felicity.

* Cf. 2 Tm 4:7-8

Startled awake and not at all hesitant about the divine message, the man went to the priest. He related the vision in the order in which it had come to him and made known what the saint had ordered. Alfred, never doubting the vision, obeyed the command. On the appointed day, once the people he had summoned had solemnly assembled, after prayers were over he with his clerics approached the place the saint had designated. They dug deeply there but found no trace of a tomb. The third hour had already come, and they had accomplished nothing. The man to whom the heavenly revelation had been made stood unwavering. By his faith he encouraged the others not

to despair. So they pressed on with their work
until the sixth hour* but saw no fruit of their
great labor.

Then not a few of the people who were standing by, wearied by the long wait, began laughing;
others, frustrated by the disappointment of such
a hope, made fun of the man for being deluded
by phantoms. Some silently blamed the priest because he had put his faith in dreams. But the man
was unmoved by them; he persevered in his con-
viction and stayed in the same place. Full of faith,
he affirmed that the body of the saint would be
found. Seizing a tool, he roused the others to dig,
those whom the delay had by now caused to slack
off, saying, 'Here, here beyond a doubt lies
Alchmund. From here we must bring up his sacred
relics today.' His great hope did not deceive him;
love did not cool in the one whose faith did not
fail. About the ninth hour,* his longed-for treasure
found, he gave substance to his promise.

When the sacred bones had been gathered
together, the venerable priest wrapped them in
absolutely clean cloths and put them in a suitable
chest. And because the late hour did not permit
the celebration of a solemn Mass, they decided
that the heavenly gift they had received should be
placed and kept that night in the eastern porch of
the church, where the memorial of Blessed Peter
the apostle used to be visited. In the silence of the
night the priest himself with his clerks kept a
sacred watch around the relics of the saint.

Inflamed by devotion, he determined to carry
some small portion of the holy bones with him
to Durham, that thus it might be lovingly cared
for and the honor paid to this saint might be increased. He thought this was owed him, that the
saint who had designated him to carry out such
a task would not refuse him a fitting reward. And
so while the others lay deep in sleep, he approached
the casket. Taking up one of the bones, a finger

that through the Creator's art had been joined by certain tendons with the interveinal nerves, he took care to lay it aside to keep it for himself.

Meanwhile dawn brought an end to the darkness of night, and the expectation of a sacred celebration excited the populace more than usual. No small crowd, made up of both sexes, assembled, desiring to be commended to the prayers of such a patron and wishing to offer some service of their own to the sacred relics. At the third hour, when all was prepared that seemed appropriate for this solemnity, the venerable priest selected those who were reckoned capable of such a task to carry the casket on their shoulders. When, approaching at the appointed time, they tried to lift the most sacred object with their hands, it remained immovable, as if fastened to the ground.

The common people, in their usual way, imputed this to the bearers' sins and declared that they should be replaced: 'Choose some others,' they said. When their attempt had no effect, the people were struck with wonder. Then, lest perhaps they too should be thought unworthy, others took their place. They too toiled in vain and then fell back without accomplishing their aim. Awestruck and agitated in mind, everyone waited for the priest's decision. Astonished and not realizing that he himself was the reason, he thought that they should spend the night in prayer and entreat the saint with the greatest devotion and request from his holiness some prophetic sign so that the reason for his immobility might not be hidden. *He spoke, and so it was done.**

* Cf. Gn 1, passim

While the clergy and people were keeping watch around the relics and praying, the saint appeared to the same man to whom he had come earlier (for sleep had overtaken him as he was watching in the church). Regarding the man severely, he said, 'What is this that you want to do? Am I to be carried to the church bereft of my members, to stand mutilated before the blessed apostle Andrew and his sacred altar, which I served for so many years with my whole body and mind?' And showing him his hand, from which half of one finger seemed to have been cut off, he said, 'Get up, and bear witness to the people that the one who took away my finger should restore it. Then my members may rest in their place of repose in their integrity, and those who have come together with such devotion to honor me may obtain the desired fruit of their labor.'

When morning came, the man got up in the midst of the people. As everyone stared at him curiously, he with a clear voice pronounced the heavenly oracle, adding that the one who had inflicted the injury on the saint should be punished with great vengeance. Then the venerable priest, although he realized that his precious token had to be restored to the saint, rejoiced that through the grace of the saint he had been found out by such a miracle. When the people had been silenced, he unhesitatingly explained everything he had done and with what intention he had done it. Once he had produced in the presence of the people what he had hidden away for himself, he restored it to its place with everyone rejoicing and reciting *God is wonderful in his saints.**   * [Ps 67:36]

When at last prayer and a fitting satisfaction had been offered, at the priest's command the clerics lifted up the bier with little effort. Accompanied by the hymns and spiritual canticles befitting such a prelate, they conveyed it into the church on the fourth nones of August.* After a   * 2 August solemn celebration of the saving sacrifice had been devoutly offered according to custom, everyone returned home with joy.

From that day forward no one dared to take anything from the sacred relics. They preserved them intact and integral, just as the brothers had found them, for the instruction of posterity. This day was celebrated every year by the people. But after the new translation had taken place, it was decreed that the renown of both saints should be celebrated in a single feast. I believe that the stories of both should be joined together, with the addition of the miracle that by the merits of the blessed man happened once on this solemnity.

13. One of the brothers, Hugh the Venerable (whom I mentioned above),[35] went to a neighboring place on monastery business and was hurrying back because of the solemnity on the next day. He had in his company a certain faithful and devout servant of the church, who was very helpful to the brothers in everything they asked of him. As they came to the river that flowed beneath the city, seated in a boat that also held some horses, Uthred (for that was the man's name) took the helm and, standing in the back, guided the boat. But suddenly—look!—a horse starting up at the front almost sank the boat under the water. Rearing vigorously on its hind legs, the beast pushed the prow down into the depths. Resurfacing immediately by reason of its lightness, the prow rose high, submerging the part where the helmsman sat. He fell from the poop and was engulfed by the river.

The onlookers cried out; they ran up, lamented, and dashed here and there, protesting his misfortune with sighs and tears. But what could they do? They had no rope, no pole, no oar, nor anything at all by which they could help the unfortunate man. They could only grieve while he was hidden under the water. Since hope alone remained, they raised their eyes to the church and besought the merits of the saints to be with them. They prayed especially to blessed Alchmund, to

---

[35] Cf. chapter 4 above, where he is called Bearded Hugh.

whose feast they had been hastening, to rescue him from these dangers.

Meanwhile the young man, whom they supposed already drowned, was submerged in the depths, his memory undiminished and his senses undisturbed. He clearly understood everything that was being said on the bank. He made his confession to the One who is everywhere present as if speaking to a priest. At last, turning his full attention to blessed Alchmund as far as his circumstances allowed, he begged him to take pity on him.

Those who were running about on the bank thought that they would be pulling out and burying a corpse, but look! they saw a man standing at a distance, holding a lance in his hand, and looking surprised at their running to and fro. They all called to him to come near, and he ran to them without delay. He thrust his single lance into the waves where the young man had last been seen, and he, seeing it at once and being conscious, seized it with both hands. His weight was a sign that the corpse was found. The others ran to help, and, see, emerging from the depths the man came onto the bank.

After resting there a little while and spitting out the water he had swallowed, he hurried with his companions to the monastery. There he was placed close to the fire, and when the natural heat that the cold had taken from his limbs had returned by means of his nearness to material fire, with his strength regained, he entered the church to give thanks to God and Saint Alchmund. There he so regained his health by the merits of blessed Alchmund that on that very day he crossed the stream and returned safe and sound to his home. From then on, as long as he lived, he came every year to the church on that day with an offering. He did not neglect to make a suitable return to his rescuer with what gifts he could for the help he had received.

Now that this has been inserted, perhaps not without profit, let us return to our account of the translation.

14. When they came to the third saint and found him buried with no less honor, they looked for a document that would give his name and merit. And, see, they found one containing these words: IN THE YEAR 766 FROM THE LORD'S INCARNATION, FRETHBERT, HIGH PRIEST OF THE CHURCH OF HEXHAM, JOURNEYED FROM THIS MORTAL FLESH TO THE TIMELESS EXISTENCE OF THE TRUE LIGHT, ON THE TENTH CALENDS OF JANUARY,* IN THE THIRTY-FOURTH YEAR OF HIS EPISCOPATE. HERE HE IS IN PEACE. When this attestation had been renewed, as in the former cases, they put him, honorably wrapped, with the others whom they had examined.

* 23 December

When they had investigated the riches of the fourth bundle in the same way, they found bones shining with no less beauty than the others, stored up and wrapped with the same care. Why the one who buried them did not put a name on them we do not know—perhaps it was because the common people all knew that there had been four bishops, whose names were not hidden from them. Many years before this translation, when I was still a boy, the whole populace unhesitatingly claimed that Acca, Alchmund, Frethbert, and Tilbert were resting there together. Perhaps, therefore, after setting down three names he believed it enough and thought that, with the others named, no one could think that the fourth was other than Tilbert. Once these four had been wrapped in precious cloths with great devotion, as they had found them together, so they placed them together in a larger casket.

Afterwards, when they opened the chest where the relics of the venerable bishop Eata were enclosed, they found his bones emitting a heavenly fragrance. When all those who were present, alarmed and stunned, had taken it in, dissolving in tears they commended themselves to the prayers of so great a patron. In the same casket they found a leaden urn containing some small bits of blessed Frethbert and giving off the same fragrance. Then thanksgiving and praise sounded in every mouth. Bringing a smaller casket, which they had ornamented, they put into it the relics of the blessed bishop along with the leaden urn they had found. When the inside had been similarly ornamented, they placed there some part of the dust of the body of Saint Acca, bishop, with the sacred relics of Saint Babylas, bishop and martyr.[36]

When a table formed of three columns and becomingly decorated with sculptures and pictures had been set up near the altar, they placed in the middle the larger chest that held the sacred tokens of the four bishops; on its southern part they set the one protecting the venerable bones of Saint Eata, and to the north they placed a third with those they had put in it.[37] When the rites had been performed and Mass celebrated with the appropriate joy, the populace was sent away, and all the brothers returned to their usual peace and quiet.

15. Someone has asked who this Eata was and at what time he governed the church at Hexham. I will not find it irksome to pass on with a pen what antiquity knew about these things or what can be proved or conjectured from the chronicles and histories. Saint Bede says this is the Eata who was once the very respected abbot of Melrose and Lindisfarne and who was worthy of having blessed

---

[36] A third-century martyred bishop of Antioch.
[37] I.e., the fragments of Frethbert, Acca, and Babylas.

Cuthbert, Saint Boisil, and many other men of great perfection as his disciples.[38]

At the time that blessed Wilfrid was in exile, King Egfrid, who had banished him, envying his renown, divided the diocese of the church of York—of which Wilfrid was the sole head—first among two bishops and afterward among three. Theodore, archbishop of Canterbury,[39] under whose authority the whole island had been placed, was well disposed toward him. To Saint Eata he committed the province of the Bernicians, establishing its seat in the church at Hexham and adding to it the governance of the church at Lindisfarne. He put Bosa over the church at York, granting to him the direction of the province of Deira. They were ordained by blessed Theodore,[40] along with the bishop of Lindsey, Eadhed.[41] After three years had passed, that same Theodore ordained Tunbert to the church at Hexham.[42] Eata, however, remained in the church at Lindisfarne. We have put this, from the history of the Venerable Bede, into our own words.*

* *Bede, HE 4.12*

Later he says that John succeeded to Eata's chair at Hexham.[43] It is clear then that after Tunbert, blessed Eata returned to his former see, with the holy father Cuthbert staying in the chair of Lindisfarne. It is said, however, that this father

---

[38] Bede identifies Boisil as prior of Melrose during Eata's abbacy and at the time of Cuthbert's entry as a novice (HE 4.27). At this point BL MS Add. 38,816 adds at the end of the first lection: 'This Eata, as Bede notes, was one of the twelve young men from the nation of the English whom the most holy Bishop Aidan first accepted for educating in Christ.'

[39] Theodore of Tarsus, archbishop of Canterbury 668–690. Bede says that Theodore was the first archbishop 'whom the whole English Church consented to obey' (HE 4.2).

[40] Theodore of Canterbury, though the manuscripts read *Theodoro Eboraci*, 'Theodore of York'.

[41] Eadhed, bishop of Lindsey 678–680.

[42] Tunbert, bishop of Hexham 681–684.

[43] John of Beverley, bishop of Hexham 687–705, archbishop of York 705–718 (cf. Bede, HE 5.2).

had been chosen for the Hexham church, but he brought it about that, with Eata returning to the see to which he had first been assigned, he himself exercised the office of bishop in the place in which he had served as a monk, choosing quiet for himself.[44] When Eata died, as Bede testifies, Saint John succeeded him.

That all these things were done while blessed Wilfrid was in exile is clear enough.[45] When he returned, John was transferred to the church at York, and Wilfrid himself received Hexham. He was transported to heaven four years after receiving the episcopate, as Michael the archangel had disclosed to him, and the most reverend Acca was his successor. This very holy Acca was ordained bishop in the see of Hexham, even though the bishop was living. Bede describes him as an extremely mild and simple man who ended his life there.* I think I ought to insert in this work a modern incident concerning him.

* *Bede, HE 5.20*

16. At the time of Thomas the Younger, a man of a gentle spirit and pleasant speech, when the canons had already been introduced into the church at Hexham, many of the clergy of York were still overbearing and proud. They could hardly bear the fact that they had no memorial of any of their bishops when this church possessed Paulinus of Rochester,[46] Wilfrid of Ripon, and John of Beverley, but to remove any of these over the people's objections would be impossible. They approached the archbishop to ask if he might allow them at least the relics of blessed Eata, for

---

[44] Although Eata had been assigned to Lindisfarne and Cuthbert to Hexham, in 685 the two exchanged sees, reportedly at Cuthbert's wish.

[45] After Theodore divided the diocese of York in 678, leaving Wilfrid without a see, Wilfrid was essentially an exile until 705. Aelred's praise of Thomas here echoes that of Symeon (Kings, AD 1114).

[46] Paulinus, bishop of York 625–633, bishop of Rochester 633–644.

the undistinguished church at Hexham possessed
five bishops while York had not even one. Taking
into account the powerlessness of the common
people of Hexham and the poverty of the brothers who had recently come there, they thought
they could safely use force on them.

As the bishop had a wonderfully kind dispo-
sition, he easily consented to their way of thinking. Together with the clerics who were to convey
the saint, he came to Hexham. There was no one
to refuse them, no one to open the mouth and
raise an alarm. The brothers, however, did what
they could. They were earnest in prayer and fought
with their prayers rather than swords even against
these thieves. They prostrated themselves before
the casket that preserved that heavenly treasure;
they wept, they begged him not to desert them,
not to prefer the wealth of York to their poverty,
not to desert the place that he had cherished when
alive and where his sepulcher enriched them. *The
Lord* listened to *the desires of the poor; his ear* heeded

* Ps 9:38   the preparation *of their heart.**

The [clergy of York] prepared what was
needed for the exhumation, but the Lord *laughed*
* Ps 2:4, Ps 32:10   *at* their preparations, *broke up their plan,** and de-
feated their attempt. Now the day on which they
were to set their proposal in motion had arrived.
The night before, when the bishop had retired to
his bed for quiet and sleep, he saw in a dream a man
standing beside him, wearing episcopal insignia,
grave in aspect, and emitting a tremendous light.
The bishop quailed, scarcely enduring the terror
that spread before his eyes and face. Trembling, he
awaited what the man would do. That one, looking wrathfully at him as he looked back, said this
to him: 'Why does it suit you to disturb my quiet
and to remove me from the place where I sleep
and rest with my brothers to other peoples? This
is not the Lord's will but your own presumption,
for which you will now pay the penalty.' Raising

the pastoral staff that he held in his hand, he struck Thomas's shoulder twice, and with many threats he disappeared.

Terrified by the blow, Thomas awoke with a shout. At this the clerics who were with him rose and came to him. Finding him trembling and pale, they entreated him to reveal the cause. He reported the vision, and in the morning, calling the brothers to him, he confessed his guilt and asked forgiveness. Promising that he would never again attempt anything of this kind, he requested that they offer a sacrifice of prayers for him. The brothers were much gladdened by this behavior, and the clerics, frustrated of their hope, were not a little perplexed. For three days Thomas suffered from the saint's blow; on the fourth day he was at last healed by the one who had struck him, the infirmity left him, and he left the town.[47]

---

[47] In the manuscripts the text ends here, without Aelred's usual doxology or request for prayers for his soul.

A CERTAIN
WONDERFUL MIRACLE

T O KNOW AND YET HIDE the Lord's miracles, the clear signs of his divine loving-kindness, is an aspect of sacrilege. For to deprive everyone of what can console people of the present, instruct those who come afterward, and increase the devotion of all is shameful. But the folly of many for the most part alarms us, who, concerning what is good, are either so consumed by envy or weakened by infidelity that they scarcely believe our own eyes, while any little thing that reaches their ears draws them to believe what is evil. So it is, most beloved Father, that I believe I should reveal to you as well as I can a thing wonderful and unheard of in our time. Your holy simplicity is accustomed to judge all things rightly and to suspect nothing bad of anyone without sure evidence. Let there be no doubt as to the truth of my words, because I have seen with my own eyes the things I am about to relate; moreover, everything was reported to me by women whose mature age and evident sanctity allows no reason for lying.

1. Among the monasteries of virgins that a man venerable and beloved of God, the father and priest Gilbert,[1] constructed with wondrous fervor

---

[1] Gilbert of Sempringham (*c.* 1083–1189).

in various provinces of England, is one located in the province of York, in a place surrounded by water and marshes, from which it takes its name. For it is called Watton, that is, 'wet place'.* Formerly, as the venerable priest Bede writes in his history of the English,* it was distinguished by throngs of holy women. There also the blessed bishop John* by his healing touch and prayer cured a girl almost despaired of because of an incautious blood-letting.[2]

* humida uilla

* Bede, HE 5.3

* of Beverley

Because by the efforts of the aforesaid father the ancient monastic practice was renewed in that place, so too were the ancient miracles renewed. There the handmaids of Christ, along with their daily manual labor and customary psalmody, were consecrated to spiritual duties and heavenly contemplation, so that many, as if leaving the world and all that is in it, were often transported into indescribable ecstasies, seeming to join in angelic choirs. They frequently conversed with good spirits, who sometimes reproved them, sometimes instructed them, and sometimes fortified them with what was certain and needful.

They showed so much love and concern for one another that when one died, the others did not cease praying until something certain enlightened them about either her punishment or her glorification. So it was that those who had died used to appear to the living not only, as is usual, in dreams but even visibly, to their physical eyes. Sometimes they would disclose the punishment and sometimes the glory that they had each merited.

It happened once that one among them of the highest reputation passed over into heaven when she left her body. Everyone loved her, but one especially cherished her. She was insistent in her prayers that the divine loving-kindness not

[2] John of Beverley, archbishop of York 705–721. Bede refers to the monastery as *Wetadun* (EH 5.3).

conceal the virgin's reward from her. In the course of the year, the anniversary of the day of her burial came around. The girl multiplied her usual prayers. Inflamed by longing, she was overcome by a flood of tears.

Meanwhile the Saving Offering for the departed woman's transgressions was being prepared for sacrifice; the priests followed the requisite office. Turning to the altar the virgin of Christ was granted her dearest wish. Imagine! a ray of the sun, sent down from the heights to the depths, settled itself before the altar step. She peered into it earnestly, and at once she saw the virgin whom she loved sitting in that ray, radiant in extraordinary splendor. Astounded, she became rigid; though her spirit spoke, her physical tongue was silent. While her body remained unmoving as though her senses were asleep, she pleaded as her sole desire to come nearer to the virgin so that she might see her more clearly.

At once the ray of the sun rose up from where it had stopped and came ever nearer. Resting before the face of the virgin, it offered that loving one the countenance she had longed for, so that she could contemplate it close at hand. Suffused with ineffable joy, she awaited the end of the heavenly service. When the Mass was closed by the voice of the deacon, she returned to herself, and the ray returned to the heights.

Having said this, it being outside our present subject, let us pass on to what we proposed to narrate.

2. While Henry of holy and loving memory was bishop of the church at York,[3] a certain girl,

---

[3] Henry Murdac, archbishop of York from 1147 until his death in 1153. A Cistercian, he had been abbot at Vauclair (1134–1144) and Fountains (1144–1147) before becoming archbishop. He appears below, in chapter 9, clothed in both habit and pallium.

thought to be four years old, was received to be
brought up in that same monastery at the holy
father's request. As soon as she grew out of infancy
into girlhood, she indulged in girlish wantonness.
She had no love of religion, no concern for order,
no sense of the fear of God. She had an impudent
look, unseemly speech, a wanton gait. She went
about clothed in the sacred veil, but in her actions
she exhibited nothing worthy of the habit. She
was rebuked by words but did not improve;
scolded with the switch but did not amend.

In her teachers' eyes she wasted hours indulging
in idleness or frittering them away in disorder; either
she passed her time in stories* or she persuaded
others to do some useless thing. Pressed by the discipline of the order, she was forced to preserve her
honor at least externally, though unwillingly. For
her everything depended on fear, nothing on love.[4]
As she came of age, she preferred external things
to inner, laziness to quiet, and play to industry.

* fabulis

3. Now it happened that the brothers of the monastery, to whom the care of the exterior is committed, entered the women's monastery to do
some kind of work.[5] Noticing their arrival, the
girl approached; curiously she watched their work
and their faces. Among them was a young man
handsomer in appearance than the others and in
age more appealing. The wretch cast her eyes on
him, and he fixed his attention on her. They re-
garded each other caressingly, and soon the devi-
ous serpent, entering the breast of each, insinuated
his pleasant poison throughout their vital parts.

[4] Cf. Aelred, Vita N 11.

[5] Although the first gilbertine communities had only nuns and lay sisters,
Gilbert soon added lay brothers, modeled on the cistercian *conversi,* to carry out
such heavy labor as work on the monastery buildings. Sometime after 1147,
Gilbert also introduced augustinian canons to administer the communities and
perform sacramental functions.

The thing was first done by nods, but nods were followed by signs. Eventually the silence was broken, and they spoke of the sweetness of love. They inflamed one another; they sowed in one another the seeds of delight, the kindling of desire. He was planning debauchment,* but she said afterwards that she was thinking only of love.

    Meanwhile their feelings grew stronger. They agreed with one mind on a place and time to speak more freely with each other and take more pleasure together. Rejecting therefore *the armor of light*,* they were pleased by the darkness of night. Fleeing public places, they favored more secret ones. The thoroughly wicked man gave a signal of ruin to the ruined: at the sound of the stone that the unhappy man promised to throw at either the wall or the roof of the house in which she usually stayed, she, being alerted to his arrival, might come out to him.

4. Where then, Father Gilbert, was your vigilant concern for the keeping of discipline? Where were your many delicate devices for excluding occasions of sin? Where then was your concern—so prudent, so cautious, and so acute—your watch so faithful over each door, window, and corner, that even evil spirits seemed to be denied access? One girl mocked all your diligence, Father, for *if the Lord does not guard the city, in vain do the sentries keep watch*.* Blessed man, you did everything a mortal could do, because it was necessary to do so. But as no one can correct someone whom God has condemned, so no one can save someone whom God has not saved.

    And you, unhappy girl, what are you doing? What are you thinking? Why are you pricking up your ears so attentively to the roof tiles? Where is your fear, where your love, where your reverence for this holy community? Where is your pleasant memory of the blessed bishop who committed

marginal notes:

* stuprum

* Rom 13:12

* Ps 127 [126]:1

you to this monastery? None of these calls you
back from such infamy. With all these gone, only
shameful attachment was alive in your heart. You
get up, you wretch, you go to the door. A divine
force repels your effort to go out; you tried again,
but you accomplished nothing. Withdrawing a
little, you celebrated the customary Vigils of the
Blessed Virgin with its twelve lessons. What more
should Christ have done for you that he did not
do?

     O astonishing blindness of heart! Are you try-
ing again to go out? See, like Balaam* you will
be allowed to go, according to the desires of your
heart, so that then you may carry on with your
wrongdoing.* You ought to be led away to
Babylon; there perhaps you will be cured!

    * Nm 22

    * Ps 81:12 [80:13]

5. What follows? Alas, she goes out. Close your
ears, virgins of Christ; shut your eyes. A virgin of
Christ goes out; in a little while an adulteress will
return. She goes out, and soon, *like a deluded dove,
heartless,** she is seized by the talons of a hawk.
She is thrown down, her mouth is stopped lest
she cry out, and, having been already debauched
in mind, she is debauched in body.

    * Hos 7:11

    The wicked gratification, once experienced,
compelled her to repeat it. When it began happening so frequently, the sisters wondered at the
sound they often heard and suspected deceit. She
was a special object of suspicion, as her habits had
already been suspected by them all. The flight of
the young man also increased their suspicion. For
when she had revealed to the adulterer that she
had conceived a child, he, fearing that he too
would be revealed, left the monastery and returned to the world.

6. Then the astute matrons summoned the girl.
Unable to hide it any longer, she confessed the
transgression. Amazement seized everyone who

heard what she said. Zeal immediately flamed up in their bones, and, looking at each other and striking their hands together, they rushed upon her, tearing the veil from her head. Some thought she ought to be given to the flames, others that she should be flayed alive, and others that she should be put on a stake to be burned over live coals. The older women restrained the fervor of the young. She was, however, stripped, stretched out, and whipped without mercy. A prison cell was prepared, where she was bound and enclosed. To each of her feet two rings were attached with fetters, with two chains of no small weight fastened to them. The end of one was fixed in an immense block of wood, and the end of the other pulled outside through the entryway, closed by a bolt. She was sustained on bread and water; she was fed with daily opprobrium.

Meanwhile her swelling womb developed what she had conceived. How great was everyone's grief! How great especially were the laments of the holy virgins who, fearing for their own honor, dreaded that the offense of one would be held against all. They felt as if they were exposed to all eyes to be mocked, given to all teeth to be mangled. They wept together, they wept separately, and, inflamed by their great sorrow, they rushed again upon the captive. If the older women had not spared what she had conceived, they would hardly ever have ceased from punishing her. She bore all these injuries patiently; she declared that she deserved still greater torments. She believed, nevertheless, that others would suffer no injury because of her infidelity.

They considered what was to be done. If she were to be expelled, it would redound to the infamy of them all, and if a mother, denied help, should die with her offspring, no little danger would threaten all their souls. 'If she is saved', they cried out, 'the birth cannot be hidden.' Then one of them said, 'It is best that the extremely wicked youth should be saddled with his paramour, heavy with the offspring of adultery, and that she should be left to the care of him to whose wickedness she agreed.' The unhappy girl said, 'If this can be a remedy for you, although I know it will be my ruin, you may see the young man on the night, at the hour, at the site of our wickedness, as he promised me he would come. It will be up to you then to hand me over to him. *According to the will*

* Mt 6:10

*of heaven,** so be it.' They eagerly seized upon her words. At once, breathing vengeance on the young man, they sought from her the truth in every detail. She confessed, insisting that what she had said was true.

7. Then the superior of the community, summoning some of the brothers, told them of the matter. He gave orders that, that night, one of them, his head covered with a veil, should sit in the designated place, and others should be hidden nearby to take him as he came, beat him with sticks, and

* Gn 1 passim

hold him bound. *He spoke, and so it was done.** The young man, ignorant of what was happening to her, came, worldly not only in mind but even in clothing. Burning with lust, *like a horse or a mule,*

* Ps 32 [31]:9

*without understanding,** as soon as he saw the veil he rushed at the man whom he thought to be a woman. But those who were present, bestowing a bitter remedy on him with cudgels, put out the growing fever.

The matter was referred to the virgins. At once some of them, having the zeal of God although not according to knowledge and wanting to avenge the injury to virginity, asked the brothers to give the youth to them for a short time, as if to learn some secret from him. When they had received him, they knocked him down and held him. She, that cause of all evils, was brought in as

* spectaculum

if to a performance.* They put an instrument into

her hands and compelled her unwillingly to cut
off his manhood with her own hands. Then one
of those standing by seized those things of which
he had been relieved and flung them as they
were—foul and covered with blood—into the
face of the sinful woman.

Do you see with what zeal these women,
champions of decency, burned, these persecutors
of impurity, these women who loved Christ more
than anything else? Do you see how they avenged
the injury to Christ by mutilating the man and
pursuing the woman with opprobrium and abuse?
Behold the sword of Levi, the fervor of Simeon.*   * *Gen 34:25*
These avengers of violated chastity did not think
they should spare even the circumcised. Behold
the zeal of Phineas the priest, who gained the
eternal priesthood by slaughtering fornicators.*   * *Nm 25:7-8*
Here shines out even the wisdom of Solomon,
who proclaimed a sentence of death on his own
brother, who asked for the virgin Abishag as his
concubine.* I praise not the deed but the zeal;   * *1 K 2:13-25*
I do not approve the shedding of blood, but I extol
the fervor of the holy virgins against such infamy.
What would they not endure, what would they
not do to preserve chastity, these who could do
so much to avenge it?

8. But let us return to the subject. The gelding was
returned to the brothers; the distraught woman
was thrust back into her cell. So far, wretched
woman, we have written the story of your misfortune; from now on we will tell with our pen
how the ever-merciful loving-kindness of Christ
rained down upon you, for *where sin increased, grace
increased all the more.**   * *Rom 5:20*

Now that vengeance had been exacted and
zeal had cooled, the holy virgins cast themselves
at the feet of Christ. They wept and prayed that
he would spare their place, that he would have
regard for their virginal shame, that he would put

down the infamy and drive away the danger. Daily
with prayers and tears they called on divine clem-
ency. And truly the sinful woman moved the holy
heart of Jesus with her grief and disgrace, and also
with the abuse she suffered.

O good Jesus, you who manifest your omni-
potence especially in sparing and in pitying, if
while you were present here in the flesh a miser-
able woman was once afflicted with such misery,
what would that loving breast do *in which the whole
treasury of* mercy as well as *all wisdom and knowledge
rested?** Let the just hear, let them rejoice in the
sight of God, and let them delight in gladness. Let
sinners hear, so that they never despair of the
goodness of him who so exercises justice as not
to forget mercy. You have looked down, good
Jesus, you have looked down on the great fervor
and fear of your handmaids and on the affliction
of your single sinner.

9. The child was already alive in her belly, and milk
flowed freely from her breasts. Moreover, her
womb seemed to swell so much that she thought
she would bear twins. A leaden color spread around
her eyes, and pallor came over her face; now her
breasts were empty of fluid, and after a little while
they were filled up with the usual liquid. Now the
prison cell could scarcely hold her. The necessary
things are now made ready for the birth. They take
what precautions they can for fear the infant's
weeping should betray the birth.

And look, in the silence of the dead of night,
when the poor woman had gone to sleep, she sees
in a dream standing beside her the bishop by
whom—as we said earlier—she had been committed to the divine service in that monastery. He
was clothed in the pallium and under it wore the
monastic habit. Regarding her with a severe look,
he said, 'Why is it that you curse me every day?'
Shaking with great fear, she denied it. Then the

* Col 2:3

holy man said, 'It is true. Why do you deny it?' The woman, seeing herself found out, replied, 'Truly, my Lord, because you handed me over to this monastery in which such evils have come upon me.' To this the prelate said, 'I blame you rather for this, that you have not yet acknowledged your sin to your spiritual father, as is necessary. But see to it that you confess as quickly as you can, and take this from me as a command, that you chant these psalms to Christ every day.' Giving her the numbers and names of the psalms, he immediately disappeared.* Awakening easier in mind, she committed the vision and the psalms to memory.

On the following night, when she was thought ready to give birth and the anticipation of that hour seemed bitter, she was even more afraid of the onset of the birth. Again the venerable pontiff appeared to the despairing woman in a dream, bringing with him two women of lovely visage. The prelate came up to the wretched woman and, as her head rested on her knees, covered her face with the pallium in which he was clothed, chiding her and saying: 'If you had been cleansed by a true confession you would clearly see what is being done. Now indeed you feel the benefit, but you cannot know the means and nature of the action.'

When, after a while, she raised herself, she saw the women bearing in their arms an infant wrapped in white linen, as it seemed to her, and following after the departing bishop. Startled awake, she felt no weight in her belly. She touched her body with her hands and found it entirely empty.

10. When morning came her guardians were there looking at her. They saw that her womb had shrunk, that her girlish—I will not say virginal—face had put on comeliness, and that her clear eyes had lost their leaden color. At once, as if not be-

lieving their own eyes, they asked, 'What is this? Have you added to your many sins that you have killed your infant?' And immediately they ransacked the narrow prison in which she sat in chains. Nothing was overlooked in the narrow cell, its cheap furnishings, its thin straw. 'And so, wretch', they said, 'you haven't given birth, have you?' She replied that she did not know. 'And where', they said, 'is your infant?' She answered, 'I do not know.' Recounting the vision, she insisted that she knew nothing more.

They did not believe her, being terrified by the novelty of the thing. They prodded her womb, and behold, such slimness had succeeded the swelling that you would think her belly attached to her spine. They prodded her breasts but drew no liquid from them. Not sparing her, however, they pressed harder, but they expressed nothing. They ran their fingers over each of her members, they explored everywhere, but they discovered no sign of a birth, no indication of a conception. They called others, and after them still others, and everyone found only one thing: everything was healthy, everything clean, everything lovely. They did not, however, presume to explain anything or to judge anything without the authority of the father.

She was still held in fetters: the iron still remained around her feet, and the chains clanked. Then she saw two ministers of divine mercy come to her; the one, after removing the chain that bound her so tightly, went away with his companion. The sisters, noticing in the morning that the chain was gone, marveled and asked the reason. They listened, but, not believing, they investigated every bit of her bedding. They found nothing. A little later they noticed that one of the fetters had fallen off her feet. When they found it whole, in the form in which it had come from its maker's instruments and at some distance from her feet, they marveled greatly. But why do I delay further?

She was loosed in the same way from the others; only one foot was still held in one fetter.

11. Meanwhile the holy father came and learned everything from the clear signs and very truthful witnesses. As he was a man of wonderful humility, he thought he should consult my insignificant self about it all. Therefore the servant of Christ came to our monastery. When he had secretly revealed the miracle to me, he asked that I not deny my presence to the handmaids of Christ. I gladly agreed.

When he had with the utmost kindness and graciousness received both me and the companions of my journey, we went down to that small cell within the cell where she was sitting, shut in her cavern. Many virgins and widows already stooped with age were present, powerful in wisdom and judgment, remarkable for holiness and much practice of regular discipline. When they had told us everything, I began to handle the fetter with my own hands, and I understood that without God's power she could not have been loosed from the others, nor could she be loosed from this one. Some of the women, however, not yet having overcome their fear, asked us if other fetters would have to be put on her. I forbade it, declaring it to be cruel and indicative of a lack of faith. We should rather expect and hope that he who freed her from the others would also release her from this one that still held her.*

At the father's order many other things were told us worthy of eternal memory. By them we understood that *the Lord is pleased with those who fear him*, especially *with those who hope in his mercy*.*

Commending ourselves, then, to their holy prayers, and consoling them as much as we could with the word of the Lord, we returned to our monastery *praising and glorifying the Lord for all we had heard and seen** and for what the holy virgins

* Ps 107 [106]:13-14, Ps 116 [115]:16-17; Bede, HE 4.22

* Ps 147 [146]:11

* Lk 2:20

had told us. A few days later a letter was brought to us from that venerable man, telling us that that fetter by which we had found her fastened had fallen off, and he consulted my unworthy self as to what should be done. Among other things I wrote these few words: '*What God has cleansed you* *must not call common*,* and her whom he has loosed you must not bind.'*

* *Acts 10:15*
* *Mt 16:19*

EPILOGUE

I have thought that this especially should be written to you, my dearest friend, as you are far removed from this region, that in this way I might remove any occasion of envy from the envious and yet not remain silent concerning the glory of Christ. Farewell.

Bibliography

EDITIONS AND TRANSLATIONS

Aelred of Rievaulx. *Aelredi Rievallensis Opera Omnia 1, Opera Ascetica.* Edd. Anselm Hoste and C. H. Talbot. CCCM 1. Turnhout: Brepols, 1971.

———. *Aelredi Rievallensis Opera Omnia 2, Sermones I–XLVI.* Ed. Gaetano Raciti. CCCM 2A. Turnhout: Brepols Publishers, 1983.

———. *Aelredi Rievallensis Opera Omnia 3, Sermones XLVII–LXXXIV.* Ed. Gaetano Raciti. CCCM 2B. Turnhout: Brepols Publishers, 2001.

———. *Aelredus Rievallensis Opera Omnia V, Homeliae de oneribus propheticis Isaiae.* Ed. Gaetano Raciti. CCCM 2D. Turnhout: Brepols, 2005.

———. *'Ælred of Rievaulx: The Pastoral Prayer'.* Translated by Mark DelCogliano. CSQ 37 (2002) 453–460.

———. *Aelred of Rievaulx: Treatises and the Pastoral Prayer.* CF 2. Kalamazoo: Cistercian Publications, 1971.

———. 'Ailredi Abbatis Rievallensis Historia de bello standardii tempore Stephani Regis, Genealogia regum Anglorum, Vita et miraculis Edwardi Regis et Confessoris, De quodam miraculo mirabili'. *Historiæ Anglicanæ Scriptores X.* Ed. Roger Twysden and John Selden. 2 vols. London: Cornelius Bee, 1652. 333–422.

———. 'De bello standardii tempore Stephani regis', 'Genealogia regum Anglorum', 'Vita S. Edwardi regis et confessoris', 'De sanctimoniali de Wattun'. *Beati Aelredi Rievallis abbatis. Operum pars secunda.—Historica.* PL 195:701–796.

————.'De sancti ecclesiæ Haugustaldensis'. *The Priory of Hexham: Its Chroniclers, Endowments, and Annals.* Ed. James Raine. Surtees Society 44. Durham: Andrews and Co., 1864. 173–203.

————. *The Historical Works.* Edited with an introduction by Marsha L. Dutton. Translated by Jane Patricia Freeland. CF 56. Kalamazoo: Cistercian Publications, 2005.

————. 'In translacione sancti Edwardi confessoris: The Lost Sermon by Ælred of Rievaulx Found?' Ed. and intro. Peter Jackson. Trans. Tom Licence. CSQ 40 (2005) 46–83.

————.'The Life of Ninian'. Translated by Winifrid MacQueen. *St. Nynia with a Translation of the Miracula Nynie Episcopi and the Vita Niniani.* John MacQueen. Edinburgh: Polygon Books, 1990. 102–133.

————.'The Life of S. Ninian'. *Lives of S. Ninian and S. Kentigern.* Ed. Alexander Penrose Forbes. Edinburgh: Edmonston and Douglas, 1874. 1–26.

————. *The Liturgical Sermons: The First Clairvaux Collection.* Translated by Theodore Berkeley and M. Basil Pennington. CF 58. Kalamazoo: Cistercian Publications, 2001.

————. *Mirror of Charity.* Translated by Elizabeth Connor. Introduction by Charles Dumont. CF 17. Kalamazoo: Cistercian Publications, 1990.

————.'Oratio Pastoralis'. Ed. Marsha L. Dutton. CSQ 38 (2003) 297–308.

————. 'Relatio Venerabilis Aelredi, Abbatis Rievallensis, de Standardo'. *Chronicles of the Reigns of Stephen, Henry II., and Richard I.* Ed. Richard Howlett. 3 vols. Rolls series. London, 1884–86. 3:lviii–lx, 179–199.

————.'Rule of Life for a Recluse'. Translated by Mary Paul Macpherson. *Aelred of Rievaulx: Treatises and Pastoral Prayer.* CF 2. Kalamazoo and Spencer, MA: Cistercian Publications, 1971. 41–102.

————. *Spiritual Friendship.* Translated by Mary Eugenia Laker. CF 5. Kalamazoo: Cistercian Publications, 1977.

————.'Vita Niniani ab Ailredo' and 'Eulogium Davidis ab Ailredo', *Vitæ antiquæ sanctorum qui habitaverunt in ea parte Britanniæ nunc vocata Scotia vel in ejus insulis.* Ed. Johannes Pinkerton. London: Johannis Nichols, 1789. [xix]–[xx], 1–23, 439–456.

————. 'Vita Niniani', 'Eulogium Davidis ab Ailredo', 'Officium Niniani'. *Pinkerton's Lives of the Scottish Saints.* 2 vols. Ed. W. M. Metcalfe. Paisley: Alexander Gardner, 1889. 1:9–47; 2:269–285.

Aldhelm. 'De virginitate. I. Prosa'. *Aldhelmi Opera*. Ed. Rudolf Ehwald. MGH Auctores Antiquissimi 15. Berlin: Weidmann, 1919. 209–323.

———. 'The prose *De Virginitate*'. Translated by Michael Lapidge. *Aldhelm: The Prose Works*. Michael Lapidge and Michael Herren. Ipswich: D. S. Brewer, Ltd., 1979. 59–132.

Ambrose. *Commentarius in Cantica Canticorum*. PL 15:1851–1962.

Asser. *Alfred the Great: Asser's Life of Alfred and Other Contemporary Sources*. Translated by Simon Keynes and Michael Lapidge. Harmondsworth: Penguin Books, 1983.

———. *Asser's Life of King Alfred together with the Annals of Saint Neots Erroneously Ascribed to Asser*. Ed. William Henry Stevenson. Oxford: Clarendon Press, 1904, rev. ed. 1959.

Bede. *Bede's Ecclesiastical History of the English People*. Edited and translated by Bertram Colgrave and R. A. B. Mynors. Oxford: Clarendon Press, 1969.

Cyprian of Carthage. *Epistolae*. PL 4:191–458.

Eddius Stephanus. 'Life of Wilfrid'. *The Age of Bede*. Translated by J. F. Webb. 1965; London: Penguin Books, 1988. 105–182.

Foreville, Raymonde, and Gillian Keir, edd. *The Book of St Gilbert*. Oxford Medieval Texts. Oxford: Clarendon Press, 1987.

John of Hexham. 'Prior John's Continuation of the Chronicle of Simeon'. *The Priory of Hexham: Its Chroniclers, Endowments, and Annals*. Ed. James Raine. Surtees Society 44. Durham: Andrews and Co., 1864. 107–171.

The Life of King Edward Who Rests at Westminster. Edited and translated by Frank Barlow. 2d. ed. 1962; Oxford: Clarendon Press, 1992.

Luard, Henry Richards, ed. *Lives of Edward the Confessor*. Rolls series. London: Longman, Brown, *et al.*, 1858.

Mabillon, Johannes, ed. *Acta Sanctorum Ordinis Sancti Benedicti*, saecula tertia, pars Ia. Paris, 1672.

Richard of Hexham. 'History of the Church of Hexham', 'The Acts of King Stephen and the Battle of the Standard'. *The Priory of Hexham: Its Chroniclers, Endowments, and Annals*. Ed. James Raine. Surtees Society 44. Durham: Andrews and Co., 1864. 1–106.

Soldiers of Christ: Saints and Saints' Lives from Late Antiquity and the Early Middle Ages. Ed. Thomas F. X. Noble and Thomas Head. University Park: The Pennsylvania State University Press, 1995. 1–29.

Sulpicius Severus. 'The Life of Saint Martin of Tours'. Translated F. R. Hoare. *The The Western Fathers, being the lives of SS. Martin of Tours, Ambrose, Augustine of Hippo, Honoratus of Arles, and Germanus Auxerre.* New York: Sheed and Ward, 1954; New York: Harper, 1965.

Symeon of Durham. 'Historia Regum'. *Symeonis monachi opera omnia.* Ed. Thomas Arnold. 2 vols. Rolls series 75. London: Longmans and Co., 1882–1885. 2:3–283.

————. *Libellvs de exordio atqve procvrsv istivs, hoc est Dvnhelmensis, ecclesie: Tract on the Origins and Progress of this the Church of Durham.* Edited and translated by David Rollason. Oxford: Clarendon Press, 2000.

Virgil. *Virgil's Works:* The Aeneid, Eclogues, *and* Georgics. Translated by J. W. Mackail. New York: The Modern Library, 1950.

Waddell, Chrysogonus, ed. *Narrative and Legislative Texts from Early Cîteaux,* Studia et Documenta vol. 9. Cîteaux: commentarii cisterciensis, 1999.

Walter Daniel. 'La lamentation de Walter Daniel sur la mort du Bienheureux Ailred'. Ed. Hugh Talbot. Coll 5 (1938) 9–20.

————. 'Lament for Aelred'. Trans. Jane Patricia Freeland. *The Life of Aelred of Rievaulx and the Letter to Maurice.* Edited and translated by F. M. Powicke. CF 57. Kalamazoo: Cistercian Publications, 1994. 140–146.

————. *Vita Ailredi Abbatis Rievall'.* Edited, translated, and introduced by Maurice Powicke. Oxford: Clarendon, 1950. Revised edition: *The Life of Aelred of Rievaulx and the Letter to Maurice.* Introduction by Marsha L. Dutton. CF 57. Kalamazoo: Cistercian Publications, 1994.

Studies

Abou-El-Haj, Barbara. 'Saint Cuthbert: The Post-Conquest Appropriation of an Anglo-Saxon Cult'. *Holy Men and Holy Women: Old English Prose Saints' Lives and their Contexts.* Ed. Paul E. Szarmach. Albany: SUNY Press, 1996. 177–206.

Aird, William B. *St Cuthbert and the Normans: The Church of Durham*, 1071–1153. Rochester: The Boydell Press, 1998.

Barrow, G. W. S. *The Kingdom of the Scots*. London: Edward Arnold, 1973.

Bell, David N. *An Index of Authors and Works in Cistercian Libraries in Great Britain*. CS 130. Kalamazoo: Cistercian Publications, 1992.

Bonner, Gerald, David Rollason, and Clare Stancliffe, eds. *St Cuthbert, His Cult and His Community to AD 1200*. Woodbridge [UK]: The Boydell Press, 1989.

Burton, Pierre-André. *Bibliotheca Aelrediana Secunda: Une bibliographie cumulative (1962–1996)*. Fédération Internationale des Instituts d'Études Médiévales, Textes et Études du Moyen Âge 7. Louvain-La-Neuve, 1997.

Constable, Giles. 'Aelred of Rievaulx and the Nun of Watton'. *Medieval Women*. Ed. Derek Baker. Oxford: Blackwell, 1978. 205–226.

Dutton, Marsha L. 'The Cistercian Source: Aelred, Bonaventure, and Ignatius'. *Goad and Nail: Studies in Medieval Cistercian History*, 10. Ed. E. Rozanne Elder. CS 84. Kalamazoo: Cistercian, 1985. 151–178.

————. 'The Conversion and Vocation of Aelred of Rievaulx: A Historical Hypothesis'. *England in the Twelfth Century*. Ed. Daniel Williams. London: Boydell Press, 1990. 31–49.

————. 'Friendship and the Love of God: Augustine's Teaching in the *Confessions* and Aelred of Rievaulx's Response in *Spiritual Friendship*'. ABR 56 (2005) 3–40.

————. 'A Historian's Historian: The Place of Bede in Aelred's Contributions to the New History of his Age'. *Truth as Gift: Studies in Cistercian History in Honor of John R. Sommerfeldt*. Edd. Marsha L. Dutton, Daniel M. La Corte, and Paul Lockey. CS 204. Kalamazoo: Cistercian, 2004. 407–448.

————. 'A Prodigal Writes Home: Aelred of Rievaulx's *De institutione inclusarum*'. *Heaven on Earth: Studies in Medieval Cistercian History, IX*. Ed. E. Rozanne Elder. CS 68. Kalamazoo: Cistercian Publications, 1983. 35–42.

Fleming, John V. *Reason and the Lover*. Princeton: Princeton University Press, 1984.

Foster, Meryl. 'Custodians of St Cuthbert: The Durham Monks' Views of their Predecessors 1083–c. 1200'. *Anglo-Norman*

Durham 1093–1193. Ed. David Rollason, Margaret Harvey, and Michael Prestwich.Woodbridge:The Boydell Press, 1994. 53–65.

Freeman, Elizabeth. *Narratives of a New Order: Cistercian Historical Writing in England, 1150–1220.*Turnhout: Brepols, 2002.

————.'The Many Functions of Cistercian Histories Using Aelred of Rievaulx's *Relatio de Standardo* as a Case Study'. *The Medieval Chronicle: Proceedings of the 1st International Conference on the Medieval Chronicle.* Ed. Erik Kooper. Amsterdam; Atlanta: Rodopi, 1999. 124–132.

————.'Nuns in the Public Sphere:Aelred of Rievaulx's *De Sanctimoniali de Wattun* and the Gendering of Authority'. *Comitatus* 17 (1996) 55–80.

Golding, Brian. *Gilbert of Sempringham and the Gilbertine Order c. 1130–c. 1300.* Oxford: Clarendon Press, 1995.

Gron, Ryszard, 'Examples of the "Good Death" in Aelred of Rievaulx', CSQ 41 (2006) 421–441.

Heffernan,Thomas J. *Sacred Biography: Saints and their Biographers in the Middle Ages.* New York and Oxford: Oxford University Press, 1988.

Hoste, Anselm. *Bibliotheca Aelrediana.* Instrumenta Patristica 2.The Hague: Nijhoff, 1962.

Karkov, Catherine E.'The Anglo-Saxon Genesis:Text, Illustration, and Audience'. *The Old English Hexateuch:Aspects and Approaches.* Ed. Rebecca Barnhouse and Benjamin C.Withers. Publications of the Richard Rawlinson Center. Kalamazoo:The Medieval Institute, 2000. 201–237.

Knowles, David. 'The Case of St William of York'. *The Historian and Character.* Cambridge: Cambridge UP, 1963. 76–97.

McGuire, Brian Patrick. *Aelred of Rievaulx: Brother and Lover.* New York: Crossroad, 1994.

Nicholl, Donald. *Thurstan:Archbishop ofYork.*York: Stonegate, 1964.

Raciti, Gaetano. 'The Preferential Option for the Weak in the Ælredian Community Model'. CSQ 32 (1997) 3–23.

Raine, James, ed. *The Priory of Hexham: Its Chroniclers, Endowments, and Annals.* Surtees Society 44. Durham: Andrews and Co., 1864.

Ridyard, S. J. '*Condigna Veneratio:* Post-Conquest Attitudes to the Saints of the Anglo-Saxons'. *Anglo-Norman Studies* 9 (1986) 179–206.

Rollason, David. 'Hagiography and Politics in Early Northumbria'. *Holy Men and Holy Women: Old English Prose Saints' Lives and their Contexts.* Ed. Paul E. Szarmach. Albany: SUNY Press, 1996. 95–114.

Ryder, Peter F. *The Two Towers of Hexham: Hexham Moot Hall and the Old Gaol.* Newcastle upon Tyne: Society of Antiquaries of Newcastle upon Tyne, 1995.

Sommerfeldt, John R. *Aelred of Rievaulx On Love and Order in the World and the Church.* New York/Mahwah, NJ: The Newman Press, 2006.

———. *Aelred of Rievaulx: Pursuing Perfect Happiness.* New York/ Mahwah, NJ: The Newman Press, 2005.

Squire, Aelred. *Aelred of Rievaulx: A Study.* London: SPCK, 1969, 1973. CS 50. Kalamazoo: Cistercian Publications, 1981.

Indices

The following abbreviations have been used in the indices:

Vita N	The Life of Ninian
SS Hag	The Lives of the Saints of Hexham
Mira	A Certain Wonderful Miracle

Index A: Table of Scriptural References

Column one indicates the scriptural reference, column two identifies the historical work and section number in which the reference appears, and column three indicates the number of the page or pages on which the reference appears in this volume. Citations to the Vulgate are in brackets.

1 Corinthians		
3:12	*Vita N* 2	44
15:53	*SS Hag* 6	81

2 Corinthians		
11:29	*Vita N* 11	57

Galatians		
5:15 cf.	*Vita N* 9	53

Ephesians		
1:18 cf.	*SS Hag* 2	74
2:2 cf.	*SS Hag* 2	73
6:14, 16–17 cf.	*Vita N* 6	48

Philippians		
1:22–24 cf.	*Vita N* 11	57

Colossians		
2:3 cf.	*Mira* 8	118
	Vita N 2	42
	Vita N 11	57

1 Timothy		
1:5	*SS Hag* 4	76
4:12 cf.	*Vita N* 2	44

2 Timothy		
4:7–8 cf.	*SS Hag* 12	96

Hebrews		
6:7–8	*Vita N* 4	45
11:13–16 cf.	*Vita N* Prol	37

James		
4:9 cf.	*Vita N* 5	46

1 Peter		
3:12 cf.	*SS Hag* 2	72

1 John		
2:16 cf.	*Vita N* 4	44

Index B: Table of Non-Scriptural References

Column one indicates the scriptural reference, column two identifies the historical work and section number in which the reference appears, and column three indicates the number of the page or pages on which the reference appears in this volume. Citations to the Vulgate are in brackets.

137

Index C: Table of People and Places

Column one indicates the scriptural reference, column two identifies the historical work and section number in which the reference appears, and column three indicates the number of the page or pages on which the reference appears in this volume. Citations to the Vulgate are in brackets.